KING LEAR

By WILLIAM SHAKESPEARE

Preface and Annotations by
HENRY N. HUDSON

Introduction by
CHARLES HAROLD HERFORD

King Lear
By William Shakespeare
Preface and Annotations by Henry N. Hudson
Introduction by Charles Harold Herford

Print ISBN 13: 978-1-4209-5334-3
eBook ISBN 13: 978-1-4209-5335-0

Cover Image: A detail of "King Lear and the Fool in the Storm, Act III Scene 2" from 'King Lear' by William Shakespeare (1564-1616) 1836 (oil on canvas), Boulanger, Louis (1806-67) / Musee de la Ville de Paris, Musee du Petit-Palais, France / Bridgeman Images.

Please visit *www.digireads.com*

CONTENTS

KING LEAR

ACT I.

ACT II.

ACT III.

ACT IV.

ACT V.

Preface

First heard of through an entry at the Stationers', dated November 26, 1607, and reading as follows: "A book called Mr. William Shakespeare's History of King Lear, as it was played before the King's Majesty at Whitehall, upon St. Stephen's night at Christmas last, by his Majesty's Servants playing usually at the Globe on the Bankside." This ascertains the play to have been acted on the 26th of December, 1606. Most likely the play had become favourably known on the public stage before it was called for at the Court. On the other hand, it contains divers names and allusions evidently borrowed from Harsnet's *Declaration of Popish Impostures*, which appeared in 1603. This is all the positive information we have as to the date of the writing.

There are, however, several passages in the play itself, referring, apparently, to contemporary events, and thus indicating still more nearly the time of the composition. Of these it seems hardly worth the while to note more than one. In Act 1., scene 2, Gloster says, "These late eclipses in the Sun and Moon portend no good to us: though the wisdom of nature can reason it thus and thus, yet nature finds itself scourged by the sequent effects." A great eclipse of the Sun took place in October, 1605, and had been looked forward to with dread as portending evil; the more so, because an eclipse of the Moon occurred within the space of a month previous. And John Harvey had, in 1588, published a book wherein, with "the wisdom of nature," he had reasoned against the common belief, that such natural events were ominous of disaster, or had any moral significance whatever. To all which, add that in November, 1605, the dreadful secret of the Gunpowder Plot came to light, so that one at all superstitiously inclined might well say that "nature finds itself scourged by the sequent effects," and that "machinations, hollowness, treachery, and all ruinous disorders follow us disquietly to our graves": putting all this together, we have ample ground for inferring the play to have been written when those events were fresh in the public mind. This of course brings down the date of composition at least to near the close of the year 1605.

The tragedy was printed at least twice, some editors say three times, in the year 1608, the form being in each case a small quarto. It also reappeared, along with the other plays, in the folio of 1623. Considerable portions of the play, as given in the quartos, are omitted in the folio; in particular one whole scene, the third in Act IV., which, though perhaps of no great account on the stage, is, in the reading, one of the sweetest and loveliest in all Shakespeare. This naturally infers the folio to have been printed from a playhouse copy in which the play had been cut down, to abridge the time of performance.—I must add that the play has several passages which were most certainly not written by Shakespeare. Two of these have considerable length, one including seventeen lines, the other fourteen. By whom they were written, and why they were inserted, it were probably vain to speculate. All such interpolations, so far as I am clear about them, are here distinguished by having asterisks set before the lines.

The story of King Lear and his three daughters is one of those old legends with which Mediaeval Romance peopled the "dark backward and abysm of time," where fact and fancy appear all of one colour and texture. In Shakespeare's time, the legendary tale which furnished the main plot of this drama was largely interwoven with the popular literature of Europe. It is met with in various forms and under various names. The oldest extant version of it, in connection with British 'history, is in Geoffrey of Monmouth, a Welsh monk of the twelfth century, who translated it from the ancient British tongue into Latin. From thence it was abridged by the Poet's favourite chronicler, Holinshed. I give a condensed statement of the Holinshed version.

Leir, the son of Baldud, was admitted ruler over the Britons in the year of the world 3105. He was a prince of right-noble demeanour, governing his land and subjects in great wealth. He had three daughters, named Gonorilla, Regan, and Cordilla, whom he greatly loved, but the youngest, Cordilla, far above the two elder. When he was come to great age, he thought to understand the affections of his daughters, and to prefer her whom he best loved to the succession. Therefore he first asked Gonorilla, the eldest, how well she loved him. She, calling her gods to witness, protested that she loved him more than her own life, which by right and reason should be most dear to her. Being well pleased with this answer, he demanded of the second how well she loved him. She answered, confirming her saying with great oaths, that she loved him more than tongue could -express, and far above all other creatures in the world. Then he called Cordilla before him, and asked what account she made of him. She answered as follows: "Knowing the great love and fatherly zeal which you have always borne towards me, I protest that I have loved you ever, and while I live shall love you, as my natural father; and, if you would understand more of the love I bear you, assure yourself that so much as you are worth, so much I love you, and no more."

The father, being nothing content with this answer, married his two eldest, the one to the Duke of Cornwall named Henninus, the other to the Duke of Albania called Maglanus; and willed that his land should be divided betwixt them after his death, and that one-half thereof should be immediately assigned to them; but for Cordilla he reserved nothing. Yet it happened that one of the Princes of Gallia whose name was Aganippus, hearing of the beauty, womanhood, and good dispositions of Cordilla, desired her in marriage; to whom answer was made that he might have her, but could have no dower, for all was promised to her sisters. Aganippus, notwithstanding this answer, took her for wife, only moved thereto by respect for her person and amiable virtues.

After Leir was fallen into age, the Dukes that had married his two elder daughters rose against him in arms, and reft from him the government of the land. He was put to his portion, that is, to live after a rate assigned to him, which in process of time was diminished. But his greatest grief was from the unkindness of his daughters, who seemed to think that what their father had was too much, the same being ever so little. Going from the one to the other, he was brought to such misery, that in the end he fled the land, and sailed into Gallia, to seek some comfort of Cordilla, whom before he hated. The lady, hearing he was arrived in poor estate, first sent him privily a sum of money, to apparel himself withal, and to retain a number of servants that might attend upon him. She then appointed him to come to the Court; which he did, and was so honourably and lovingly received, that his heart was greatly comforted: for he was no less honoured than if he had been king of the whole country. Aganippus also caused a mighty army to be put in readiness, and a great navy of ships to be rigged, to pass over into Britain with his father-in-law. When this army and navy were ready, Leir and his daughter, with her husband, took the sea, and, arriving in Britain, fought with their enemies, and discomfitted them in battle, Maglanus and Henninus being slain. Leir was then restored to his kingdom, which he ruled for the space of two years after this, and then died, forty years after he first began to reign.

The same story, with certain variations, is told briefly by Spenser in *The Faerie Queene*, book ii., canto Io; also, at much more length, in a versified form written by John Higgins, and published in *The Mirror for Magistrates*; also in an old ballad, printed in Percy's *Reliques*: but this latter was probably subsequent to the tragedy, and partly founded upon it. It appears, also, by an entry at the Stationers', dated May 14, 1594, that there was an older play on the same subject. Finally, a play, entitled "The True Chronicle History of King Leir and his three Daughters," was entered at the Stationers', May 8, 16o5, and published. Possibly this may have been another play than that heard of in 1594, but probably it was the same. Be this as it may, the piece is a wretched thing, and cannot be supposed to have contributed any thing towards Shakespeare's tragedy, unless it may have suggested to him the theme.

Thus much as to what the Poet had before him for the main plot of *King Lear*. The subordinate plot of Gloster and his sons was doubtless partly founded upon an episodical chapter in Sir Philip Sidney's *Arcadia*, entitled "The pitiful state and story of the Paphlagonian unkind King and his kind son; first related by the son, then by the blind father." Of this', also, I give a condensed statement.

The "Princes" who figure in Sidney's work, being overtaken by a furious storm, are forced to seek shelter in a hollow rock, where, themselves unseen, they overhear a dialogue between an aged man and a young, both poorly arrayed, extremely weatherbeaten; the old man blind, the young man leading him. At length, the talk became so sad and pitiful, that the princes were moved to go out to them and ask the younger what they were. He answered, "Sirs, I see well you are strangers, that know not our misery, so well known here. Indeed our state is such that, though nothing is so needful to us as pity, yet nothing is more dangerous unto us than to make ourselves so known as may stir pity. This old man, lately rightful Prince of this country of Paphlagonia, was, by the hard-hearted ungreatfulness of a son of his, deprived not only of his kingdom, but of his sight, the riches which Nature grants to the poorest creatures. By this and other unnatural dealings he hath been driven to such grief, that even now he would have me lead him to the top of this rock, thence to cast himself headlong to death; and so would have made me, who received my life from him, to be the worker of his destruction. But, noble gentlemen, if either of you have a father, and feel what dutiful affection is engrafted in a son's heart, let me entreat you to convey this afflicted Prince to some place of rest and security."

Before they could make answer, the father began to speak. "Ah, my son," said he, "how evil an historian are you, that leave out the chief knot of all the discourse, my wickedness, my wickedness! If thou doest it to spare my ears, assure thyself thou dost mistake me. I take to witness that Sun which you see, that nothing is so welcome to me as the publishing of my shame. Therefore know you, gentlemen, that whatsoever my son hath said is true. But, besides, this also is true, that, having had in lawful marriage this son, I was carried by a bastard son of mine, first to mislike, then to hate, lastly to do my best to destroy this son. If I should tell you what ways he used, to bring me to it, I should tediously trouble you with as much poisonous hypocrisy, desperate fraud, smooth malice, hidden ambition, and smiling envy, as in any living person could be harboured. But no remembrance of naughtiness delights me but mine own; and methinks the accusing his traps might in some manner excuse my fault, which I loathe to do. The conclusion is, that I gave order to some servants of mine to lead this son out into a forest, and there to kill him.

"But those thieves spared his life, letting him go to live poorly; which he did, giving himself to be a private soldier in a country near by. But, as he was ready to be greatly advanced for some noble service which he did, he heard news of me; who suffered myself to be so governed by that unlawful and unnatural son, that, ere I was aware, I had left myself nothing but the name of a king. He, soon growing weary even of this, threw me out of my seat, and put out my eyes; and then let me go, neither imprisoning nor killing me, but rather delighting to make me feel my misery. And as he came to the crown by unjust means, so he kept it as unjustly; disarming all his own countrymen, so that no man durst show so much charity as to lend me a hand to guide my dark steps; till this son, forgetting my abominable wrongs, and neglecting the way he was in of doing himself good, came hither to do this kind office which you see him performing towards me, to my unspeakable grief. Above all, it grieves me that he should desperately adventure the loss of his life for mine, as if he would carry mud in a chest of crystal: for well I know, he that now reigneth will not let slip any advantage to make him away, whose just title may one day shake the seat of a never-secure tyranny. For this cause I craved of him to lead me to the top of this rock, meaning to free him from so serpentine a companion as I am. But he, finding what I purposed, only therein since he was born showed himself disobedient to me. And now, gentlemen, you have the true story; which I pray you publish to the world, that my mischievous proceedings may be the glory of his filial piety, the only reward now left for so great merit."

HENRY HUDSON

1881.

Introduction

The first edition of *King Lear*, in Quarto (Q₁), was printed in 1608, and has the following title-page:—

M. William Shak-speare: | HIS | True Chronicle Historie of the life and | death of King LEAR and his three | Daughters. | *With the unfortunate life of* Edgar, *sonne* | and heire to the Earle of Gloster, and his | sullen and assumed humor of | TOM of Bedlam: | *As it was played before the Kings Maiestie at Whitehall upon* | *S.* Stephans *night in Christmas Hollidayes.* | By his Maiesties seruants playing usually at the Gloabe | on the Bancke-side. | LONDON, | Printed for *Nathaniel Butter*, and are to be sold at his shop in *Pauls* | Churchyard at the signe of the Pide Bull neere | St. *Austins* Gate. 1608. |

Below the title is a device, identical with one used by the Frankfurt printers, Wechelum.

The bibliography of this edition is complicated by the fact that it was hastily made up of sheets which had, and of others which had not, been corrected, all the six extant copies containing from one to four uncorrected sheets, and being in only two cases alike.[1] The 'corrections' are merely those of a somewhat incompetent printer.

In the same year a second Quarto (Q₂) appeared, with a different device, and omitting the name of the place of sale. The text of Q₂

---

[1] Thus one of the two British Museum copies and one of the two Bodleian copies contain only one uncorrected sheet; the Devonshire copy, three.

follows now the corrected, now the uncorrected copies of Q_1 frequently, however, perverting both with new corrections of its own, all unauthentic and, with three or four possible exceptions, all wrong. They are of no interest for the student of Shakespeare.[2] A third Quarto was carelessly printed in 1655 from Q_2.

A graver problem concerns the relation of the Quartos to the First Folio. The circumstances resemble those of *Richard III.* The text swarms with "variations in word and phrase, and each version omits considerable passages which the other supplies. Of the variants a large number are purely indifferent,—substitutions of metrically equivalent synonyms. In a number of others the Folio corrects the palpable blunders of the Qq, many of which, however, it retains. In a third, smaller, group the Qq seem to give the genuine version, the Ff a diffuse perversion of it which had gained a vogue on the stage.[3] About 50 lines occur in the Folio for the first time.[4] On the other hand, the Ff omit some 220 lines found in Qq.[5] Of the authenticity of all the passages peculiar to either text there cannot be a doubt, and there is a strong *prima facie* probability that all are derived from the same original version, so long a play being inevitably curtailed in performance. The omissions in Ff are certainly due to such curtailment, whether this be ascribed to Shakespeare himself, with Koppel,[6] or, with Delius,[7] to

---

[2] Of considerable interest, however, for the student of Shakespeare's public. A pithy phrase of Goneril's (iv. 2. 28), *e.g.*, underwent the following transformations:—

    (1) Q_1 (with sheet uncorrected):
        My foote usurpes my body.
    (2) Q_1 (with sheet H uncorrected):
        A foole usurpes my bed.
    (3) Q_2:
        My foote usurpes my head.
    The Folio first gave the accepted text:
        My foole usurpes my body.
        Prætorius: Facsimiles of Q_1 and Q_2, Introduction.

Equally curious was the fate of Kent's 'Nothing almost sees miracles but miserie' (ii. 2. 172). In the uncorrected Q_1 this is given as: 'Nothing almost sees my rackles but,' etc. The 'corrected' Q_1 amends 'my rackles' to 'my wrackle,' and this is followed by Q_2.

[3] Thus, in ii. 2. 152: (of Kent in the stocks) Qq 'the king must take it ill,'—is expanded in Ff (against metre) to 'the king his master needs must take it ill.'

[4] The chief of these are: ii. 4. 142-147 (*Say. . . blame*); iii. 2. 79-95 (*This. . .time*); iv. 1. 6-9 (*Welcome. . .blasts*).

[5] The chief of these are: i. 3. 16-20 (*Not to be. . . abused*); i. 4. 154-169 (*That lord . . . snatching*); 252-256 (*I would learn . . . father*); ii. 2. 148-152 (*His fault. . . are punish'd with*); iii. 1. 7-15 (*tears . . . take all*); 30-42 (*But, true . . . to you*); iii. 6. 17-59 (*The foul . . . 'scape*); iv. 3.; v. 1. 23-28 (*Where I. .. nobly*); iv. 2. 31-50 (*I fear . . . deep*); v. 3. 54-59 (*At this time . . . place*); 204-221 (*This. . . slave*).

[6] *Text-kritische Studien über Richard III. u. King Lear* (1877).

[7] *Ueber den ursprünglichen Text des King Lear (Jahrbuch* x. 50 f.). Delius replied to Koppel in *Anglia* i. (chiefly with reference to *Richard III.*).

irresponsible actors.[8] The additions in the Ff are more difficult to judge. Some of them may be referred, as Delius would refer all, to the palpably careless printer.[9] Others may be passages hastily cut out in the early acting version, but afterwards restored. The theory of a subsequent Shakespearean revision cannot be absolutely dismissed. If Shakespeare in his ripest maturity patched *King Lear*, his art was probably quite a match for our tests, as it hardly is in the patching of *Love's Labour's Lost*. But a study of the variants rather suggests that they can be wholly explained from the twofold operation of blundering printers (in Qq) and semi-intelligent actors (in Ff). Doubtless they have sometimes co-operated to deprive us of Shakespeare's phrases altogether. No dogmatic opinion can be pronounced; but the hypothesis, on the whole, works well, that the play was first badly printed (in Qq) from a MS. slightly abridged for the performance at Court; subsequently well printed (in the Folio) from a copy of Q2 rather carelessly corrected by the more severely abridged and amended stage MS.

The date of *King Lear* may be fixed with some certainty in 1605-6. An entry in the Stationers' Register, under Nov. 26, 1607, shows that it was 'played before the Kings Majesty at Whitehall upon S. Stephens night at Christmas last,' *i.e.* on Dec. 26, 1606. Phenomenal events had marked the autumn of the previous year: in October, a great eclipse of the sun; in November, the appalling plot of Guy Fawkes. Gloster's faith that 'these eclipses do portend these divisions,' and Edmund's ridicule of it, can hardly be detached from circumstances in which this 'excellent foppery of the world' must have been peculiarly rife. In no case can the drama have been written before 1603, the names of Edgar's fiends being taken from Harsnett's *Declaration of Popish Impostures*, published in that year.

---

[8] Some of the passages excised are necessary for comprehension, *e.g.* iii. 1. 30-42 (the account of the French invasion); or for the consistency of the context, *e.g.* St. 2. 31-50 (Albany's reproof of Goneril); in Ff her 'Milk-liver'd man,' v. 50, appears unprovoked; others belong to the high poetry of the play rather than to its dramatic mechanism. It is hard to believe that Shakespeare could have cut out the trial of Goneril (iii. 6. 17-59).

[9] Thus in ii. 4. 22 (the rapid colloquy of Lear with Kent in the stocks)—

> *L.* By Jupiter, I swear, no.
> *K. By Juno, I swear, ay* (omitted in Qq).
> *L.* They durst not do't—

the compositor's eye seems to have been misled by the similarity of Kent's speech to Lear's. In other cases a longer but still more necessary speech has clearly dropped out.

Thus, in the dialogue of the Fool with Lear in iii. 6. 10f., Qq give the Fool's question: 'Prithee, nuncle, tell me whether a madman be a gentleman or a yeoman?' and Lear's wonderful: 'A king, a king!' but omit the Fool's comment; 'No, he's a yeoman that has a gentleman to his son,' etc.

Lear (Leir, Llyr), tenth king of Britain 'in the year of the world 3105, at what time Joas reigned in Juda,' was a familiar name to the Elizabethans. As undisputed history his legend had been transcribed by successive chroniclers, in prose and verse, from Layamon to Holinshed (1577); as a dramatic story, with a telling moral, it had attracted the compilers of the *Gesta Romanorum* and of the *Mirror for Magistrates*. In Higgins' supplementary First Part of that popular repertory of tragic tales (1574) 'Queen Cordila' told her father's fate and her own. Spenser, a little later, epitomised the story in half a dozen stanzas of the *Faerie Queene* (bk. ii. c. x. 27-32). Finally, in 1592-3, an unknown hand dramatised it as 'The Chronicle Historie of King Leir and his Three Daughters.' The play was entered in the Stationers' Register, 1594, but first printed in 1605, with a title-page calculated to identify it with the great tragedy then in the first splendour of its fame. The ultimate source of all these versions is Geoffrey of Monmouth's *Historia Britonum*, founded professedly upon an old Welsh chronicle. The motive of the Love-test and the Threefold division has far-reaching affinities and parallels in folklore. Camden tells it of the West Saxon king Ina. The legend, as told in all these versions, consists of three groups of incidents. In the first, Lear puts his three daughters to the love-test, and disinherits the youngest, who fails to satisfy it. In the second, the two favoured daughters maltreat him in various ways. In the third, the disgraced daughter rescues and restores him.

The first group of incidents is evidently the kernel of the whole, but its fantastic extravagance favoured variation, and three distinct versions were current among the Elizabethans. According to the first (that of Geoffrey of Monmouth and the *Mirror for Magistrates*), Lear questions his daughters to ascertain which deserves the largest of the three prospective shares, thinking 'to guerdon most where favour most be found.'[10] According to the second (Spenser's), three *equal* shares have already been arranged, and the questions aim merely at a formal test of the competency of the heirs to inherit them. In the third version (Holinshed's), the questions are a mere disguise for the king's partiality to Cordelia: he designs to bequeath the kingdom entire, and 'preferre hir whom he best loved to the succession.'

Cordelia's reply, again, though always unsatisfactory to her father, exhibits several shades of bluntness, from the brutal '*So much as you have, so much you are worth, and so much I love you, and no more*' of Geoffrey, to the discreet declaration in the *Mirror for Magistrates*' version, that she loves him '*as I ought my father.*' Holinshed's Cordeilla accounts for her love in both ways. Camden's version alone anticipates the beautiful and cogent reason of Shakespeare's Cordelia: 'Albeit she did love . . . him and so would while she lived, as much as

---

[10] *Mirror for Magistrates*, i. 125.

duty and daughterly love at the uttermost could expect, yet she did think that one day it would come to pass that she should affect another more fervently, when she was married.'

So far, it is to be noted, there is no question of abdication. Lear has merely appointed his heirs. In Holinshed he allows the heirs to take immediate possession of half their future domains, but retains the other halves during his life. The dukes, however, grow impatient, and 'thinking it long ere the government of the land did come to their hands,' they 'arose against him in armour and reft from him the governance of the land, upon conditions to be continued for term of life.' The conditions are broken and his allowance diminished; he flies to Cordeilla in Gallia, where he is 'so joyfully, honourably and lovingly received . . . that his heart was greatly comforted.' She raises a great army and fleet, they cross over to Britain, fight a great battle in which the dukes are slain, 'and then was Leir restored to his Kingdom, which he ruled after this by the space of two years, and then died, forty years after he began to reign.' Cordeilla succeeds him, and reigns for five years; when Margan the son of Gonorilla and Cunedag the son of Ragan rebelled against her, and 'being a woman of a manly courage' she ends her life.[11]

The whole of this after-history, however, is dismissed by Holinshed with a brief summary. The core of the legend still lies for him in the dramatic incident of the Love-test. For Shakespeare this incident is a mere preliminary to the tragic plot,—a rudimentary survival important only for what it leads to. A dozen years before he wrote, the author of the old Chronicle History of *King Leir and his Three Daughters* had attempted to evoke the pathos of Lear's sufferings, in the fashion of the days when *Henry VI.* and *Edward II.* were recent. He makes some show of technique, providing fresh incidents and stronger motives for the old. Leir is seen at the outset about to abdicate his crown. The 'trial of love' is ingeniously connected with his schemes for marrying his daughters, becoming a sudden stratagem to entrap Cordelia into compliance with his wishes:—

> Then at the vantage will I take Cordeilla,
> Even as she doth protest she loves me best,
> I'll say, 'Then, daughter, grant me one request,

---

[11] The words of farewell in the Mirror for Magistrates look like a reminiscence of the then recent death of Mary:—

> Farewell my realm of Fraunce, farewell, Adieu:
> *Adieu mes nobles tous,* and England now farewell:
> Farewell Madames my Ladyes, *carie suis perdu,* etc.

Her suicide forms the climax of a long debate with 'Despair,' which perhaps suggested the great scene in book i. c. ix. of the *Faerie Queene.*

> To show thou lovest me as thy sisters do,
> Accept a husband whom myself will woo . . .
> Then will I triumph in my policy,
> And match her with a King of Brittany.'

The stratagem fails, and Cordeilla is disinherited despite the protest of Leir's faithful counsellor Perillus. As the guest of Goneril he shows himself

> the mirrour of mild patience,
> Puts up all wrongs and never gives reply.[12]

The inoffensive Leir at length flies; whereupon Goneril incenses Regan against him with a slanderous report that he 'hath detracted her and most intolerably abused me.' Regan, infuriated, commissions the 'Messenger,' a serviceable rogue, to murder Leir and Perillus. After the manner of Lightborn with Edward in the dungeon *(Edw. II.* v. 5.), or Gloster with Henry in the Tower (3 *Hen. VI.* v. 6.), he holds a catlike dialogue with the two helpless old men. At the critical moment a *deus ex machina* in the form of a clap of thunder intervenes to save them; the Messenger quakes and drops the daggers. Leir and Perillus then escape to France, and faint with hunger and exposure fall in with Cordeilla and her husband disguised as peasant folk. Slowly her identity dawns upon him, and a pathetic recognition-scene ensues. With Leir's triumphant restoration the play ends. A dozen years earlier the time-honoured tragic climax of Cordelia's death would hardly have been thus forborne.

It is clear that the author of the Chronicle play made important advances in the plot, some of which Shakespeare did not disdain to adopt. Lear, like his prototype, resigns his kingdom, and does not merely determine who shall inherit it after his death. Kent is a blunter Perillus, Oswald a less masculine 'Messenger.' Leir's reunion with Cordeilla faintly foreshadows the ineffable pathos of the close of Shakespeare's Fourth Act.[13] But beyond this, the old play interests us

---

[12] A phrase perhaps in Shakespeare's mind when he made Lear, piteously striving with his frenzy, exclaim: 'No, I will be the pattern of all patience' (iii. 2. 37).

[13]   *Cor.* Ah, good old father, tell to me thy griefe,
            He sorrow with thee, if not edde reliefe.
        Leir. Ah, good young daughter, I may call thee so;
            For thou art like a daughter I did owe.
        Cor. Do you not owe her still?
            What, is she dead?
        Leir. No, God forbid; but all my interest's gone
            By shewing myself too unnaturall:
            So have I lost the title of a father,
            And may be call'd a stranger to her rather.

chiefly as setting forth paths from which Shakespeare deliberately departed. Such guidance to the workings of Shakespeare's art and mind is here peculiarly welcome, for *King Lear* confronts us with more baffling problems than any other tragedy, hardly excepting even *Hamlet.*

To the author of *Othello*, the Leir story naturally suggested a tragedy of fateful credulity and poignant disillusion. For the imagined unfaithfulness of a wife there were the actual infidelities of children: if aught could be more pathetic than the pang of 'jealousy' which 'perplexes' and overwhelms Othello, it was the ruin wrought by the serpent's tooth of ingratitude in the yet simpler and greater heart of an old father. Such a character was already hinted in the Leir of the legend. All these germs of tragic unreason, which the painstaking and matter-of-fact older playwright did his best to eliminate, are expanded and vitalised in the wonderful, Titanically infantine, Lear of Shakespeare,—that sea where all the winds of tragedy meet in tumult.

This procedure is exhibited with peculiar daring in the much-discussed opening scene. Goethe branded it as 'irrational'; and irrational it is in so far as it throws into glaring prominence the sublime unreason of Lear. Far from rationalising the folktale *motif*, Shakespeare combines several incongruous versions of it in the chaotic purposes of the king. In some versions, as we have seen, the kingdom is to be equally divided, in others the shares are proportioned to the 'love.' It is reserved for Shakespeare's Lear after contemplating an equal division and assigning two 'ample thirds' to the elder daughters, to invite Cordelia to merit 'a third more opulent than your sisters.' In their subsequent attitude, again, the Leir of the *Chronicle*, and of the old play, were both consistent; the one had not abdicated, and therefore justly claimed his royal state; the other resigned his state with his crown. It was reserved for Shakespeare's Lear to insist upon keeping the authority of kingship after he had 'given it away.' The Leir of the old play brings no retinue to his daughter's house; the Leir of the *Mirror for Magistrates* brings sixty knights who are not described as unruly; it was reserved for Shakespeare's Lear to bring a hundred who 'hourly carp and quarrel,' and to meet resentful protests with the fierce intractable irony of his, 'Your name, fair gentlewoman ?'—the ominous premonition of the frenzy of implacable rage which burns

---

Here may be the germ of
Lear. ... As I am a man, I think this lady
    To be my child Cordelia.
Cor. And so I am, I am.
Lear. . . . your sisters
    Have, as I do remember, done me wrong:
    You have some cause, they have not.
                                    (iv. 7. 698 f.)

itself out only after consuming the vast tottering fabric of his mind,—
that 'tower sublime of yesterday, that royally did wear its crown of
weeds.'

In the splendour of that consuming flame the tragedy reaches its
climax. Lear's madness is rooted in his unreason,—it is the inevitable
fate of an intellect too rigid and untaught to find its bearings in a world
where its will is thwarted. But the shock which blurs his senses startles
into activity new faculties of apprehension and divination. Insensibly
before our eyes the proportions of things change, the irrational and
intractable old man grows into the sublime embodiment of 'a grandeur
that baffles the malice of daughters and of storms'; 'in the aberrations
of his reason we discover a mighty irregular power of reasoning,
immethodised from the ordinary purposes of life, but exerting its
powers, as the wind bloweth where it listeth, at will upon the
corruptions and abuses of mankind.'[14]

Then the lurid splendour fades, the great rage expires, and all that
is left in the ruined mind, his vehement, childlike need of love, flings
him, helpless as a child, into Cordelia's healing and upholding arms.
The gladness of her presence irradiates his mind:—

> Come, let's away to prison:
> We two alone will sing like birds i' the cage:
> And take upon's the mystery of things
> As if we were God's spies: . . .

She fans the frail spark of his existence, and with the inexorable fate
that stops her breath, it expires. Thus Shakespeare brings the old 'tragic
tale' of Cordelia's desperate death, like all the other miseries of the
story, into relation with the supreme pathos of the fate of Lear.

It was evidently as a foil to Lear's sublime agony that Shakespeare
introduced the crasser and more material Nemesis that visits the
kindred folly of Gloster. The two stories have the obtrusive parallelism
of Shakespeare's early comic plots—one of several points in which the
drama on the technical side might be described as an assemblage of
Shakespeare's discarded methods, touched to finer issues. In detail,
however, they betray at once the different quality of their origin.
Gloster's relations to Edmund and Edgar are expanded from the brief
episode, in Sidney's *Arcadia*, of the Paphlagonian 'unkind king,' who
is blinded by the son he favours, and the 'kind son' who then saves him
by Edgar's dangerously fantastic stratagem. Across the woof of an
immemorial Celtic folk-tale Shakespeare thus threw the modern fancy
arabesque of an accomplished poet, with its deliberate audacities of
horror and romance. The Gloster story echoes the theme of the Lear

---

[14] Charles Lamb.

story in a duller and more conventional key, as the Laertes story echoes the story of Hamlet. The wrongs done and suffered are more grossly and glaringly criminal; but more deserved and less pathetic Gloster's blinding far exceeds in material savagery any suffering inflicted upon Lear; but his dejected patience as he gropes with eyeless orbs towards Dover recalls only the meek suffering of the Leir of the *Chronicle*. His pangs stir in him no tempest of the mind. 'Poetic justice' is sublimely defied in the doom of Lear and of Cordelia; but Gloster is blinded by the child of his pleasant vices, and Edmund slain by the brother he has wronged. As Lear's tempest of the mind is opposed to Gloster's torments of the flesh, so the subtle malignity and blind, suicidal passion of Goneril and Regan stand in contrast with the cool, pragmatic villany of Gloster. Their common passion for him is the most salient trait added by Shakespeare to the Goneril and Regan of tradition, and the death of one at the hands of the other strikes a last fierce note from the chord of violated blood-ties that resounds through the play. But the dagger and the poison-bowl are not the habitual methods of the Shakespearean Regan and Goneril. They affect a subtler and more impalpable cruelty, conveyed through the forms of legal and speciously reasonable acts. Goneril does not, as in the old play, inflame Regan against Lear by slander, nor does Regan hire a murderer to despatch him. The exposure of Lear to the night and storm is, with wonderful art, made to appear the result of his headstrong choice. The two interwoven stories thus carry us through the whole gamut of suffering. No other tragedy is so charged with pain, so crowded with contrivers of harm. But no other is so lighted up with heroic goodness. The querulous laments of old Gloster over the 'machinations, hollowness, treachery, and ruinous disorders' of the time,—'in cities, mutinies; in countries, discord; in palaces, treason,'—express the groundwork of the tragedy, but hardly its groundtone. Anarchy is rampant, but true hearts abound,—lonely beacons of the moral order which is half effaced in the social fabric. Fidelity and frankness were the salient traits of the traditional Cordelia. Shakespeare not only gives these traits a heightened beauty in her, but repeats them, subtly varied and modulated, in a series of other characters;—in the rough-tongued, loyal Kent; in Cornwall's brave 'dunghill slave,' who insolently avenges the blinding of Gloster; and, not least, in that exquisite scherzo to Cordelia's andante—the Fool. This characteristic type of the Comedies appears nowhere else in tragedy; but in the close of the comic period we find the Fool shaping towards the functions he performs in *Lear*. Frankness was his official prerogative; fidelity his added grace. The calamities of *As You Like It* are as the passing of a summer cloud compared with those of *Lear*; but such as they are, Touchstone shares in them, throwing in his lot with his banished mistresses, and pricking their romantic extravagances with the rough-hewn bolts of his dry brain. The overwhelming pathos of *Lear* is evolved from a situation in itself quite as capable of yielding farce; and as the tragedy deepens, humour melts into pathos in the chorus-like comments of the more exquisite and finely-tempered Touchstone who follows the king into the night and storm, and vanishes from our ken, like a wild dream-fancy, when the troubled morning breaks.

CHARLES HAROLD HERFORD

1902.

KING LEAR

DRAMATIS PERSONAE.

LEAR, *King of Britain.*
KING OF FRANCE.
DUKE OF BURGUNDY.
DUKE OF CORNWALL.
DUKE OF ALBANY.
EARL OF KENT.
EARL OF GLOUCESTER.
EDGAR, *son of Gloucester.*
EDMUND, *bastard son to Gloucester.*
CURAN, *a courtier.*
OLD MAN, *tenant to Gloucester.*
DOCTOR.
LEAR'S FOOL.
OSWALD, *steward to Goneril.*
A Captain under Edmund's command.
Gentlemen.
A Herald.
Servants to Cornwall.

GONERIL, *daughter to Lear.*
REGAN, *daughter to Lear.*
CORDELIA, *daughter to Lear.*

Knights attending on Lear, Officers, Messengers, Soldiers, Attendants.

ACT I.

SCENE I.

KING LEAR's *Palace.*

[*Enter* KENT, GLOUCESTER, *and* EDMUND.]

KENT. I thought the King had more affected[1] the Duke of Albany than Cornwall.

GLOUCESTER. It did always seem so to us: but now, in the division of the kingdom, it appears not which of the dukes he values most; for equalities are so weigh'd,[2] that curiosity in neither can make choice of either's moiety.[3]

KENT. Is not this your son, my lord?

GLOUCESTER. His breeding, sir, hath been at my charge: I have so often blushed to acknowledge him, that now I am brazed to it.

KENT. I cannot conceive you.

GLOUCESTER. Sir, this young fellow's mother could: whereupon she grew round-wombed, and had, indeed, sir, a son for her cradle ere she had a husband for her bed. Do you smell a fault?

KENT. I cannot wish the fault undone, the issue of it being so proper.[4]

GLOUCESTER. But I have, sir, a son by order of law, some year elder than this, who yet is no dearer in my account: though this knave came something saucily into the world before he was sent for, yet was his mother fair; there was good sport at his making, and the whoreson must be acknowledged. Do you know this noble gentleman, Edmund?

EDMUND. No, my lord.

GLOUCESTER. My lord of Kent: remember him hereafter as my honourable friend.

EDMUND. My services to your lordship.

KENT. I must love you, and sue to know you better.

EDMUND. Sir, I shall study deserving.

---

[1] To *affect* a thing, as the word is here used, is to *take to* it, to have an *inclination* towards it.

[2] That is, the portions are weighed out or arranged so *equally*, or *in such equality.* A *proleptical* mode of speech, like many others.

[3] *Moiety* properly means half, but was used for any part or portion.—*Curiosity* is *close scrutiny,* or *scrupulous exactness.*—This speech goes far to interpret Lear's subsequent action, as it shows that the division of the kingdom has already been concluded, and the several portions allotted, and so infers the trial of professions to be a sort of pet device with the old King, a thing that has no purpose but to gratify a childish whim. The opening thus forecasts Lear's madness.

[4] Here, as usual in Shakespeare, *proper* is *handsome,* or *fine-looking.*

GLOUCESTER. He hath been out nine years, and away he shall again.[5]—[*Sennet Within.*] The King is coming.

[*Enter* KING LEAR, ALBANY, CORNWALL, GONERIL, REGAN, CORDELIA, *and* ATTENDANTS.]

KING LEAR. Attend the lords of France and Burgundy, Gloucester.
GLOUCESTER. I shall, my liege.

[*Exeunt* GLOUCESTER *and* EDMUND.]

KING LEAR. Meantime we shall express our darker purpose.[6]—
    Give me the map there.—Know that we have divided
    In three our kingdom: and 'tis our fast intent
    To shake all cares and business from our age;
    Conferring them on younger strengths, while we
    Unburthen'd crawl toward death.—Our son of Cornwall,
    And you, our no less loving son of Albany,
    We have this hour a constant will[7] to publish
    Our daughters' several dowers, that future strife
    May be prevented now.[8] The princes, France and Burgundy,
    Great rivals in our youngest daughter's love,
    Long in our court have made their amorous sojourn,
    And here are to be answer'd.—Tell me, my daughters,—
    Since now we will divest us both of rule,
    Interest of territory, cares of State,—
    Which of you shall we say doth love us most?
    That we our largest bounty may extend
    Where nature doth with merit challenge.[9]—Goneril,
    Our eldest-born, speak first.
GONERIL. Sir, I love you more than words can wield the matter;[10]

---

[5] As Edmund's villainy is a leading force in the dramatic action, an intimation of the causes which have been at work preparing him for crime is judiciously given here in the outset of the play.—Gloster's meaning in this last Speech clearly is, that he has kept Edmund *away from home* nine years, and intends sending him away again, in order to avoid the shame of his presence, or because he has so "often blush'd to acknowledge him." We may Suppose Edmund's absence to have been spent in travelling abroad, or in pursuing his studies, or in some kind of foreign service. And this accounts for his not being acquainted with Kent.

[6] Lear's "darker purpose" is probably that of surprising his daughters into a rivalry of affection. This he has hitherto *kept dark* about; though his scheme of dividing the kingdom was known, at least in the Court.

[7] "*Constant* will" is *fixed* or *determined* will; the same as "*fast* intent."

[8] "That future strife may be prevented *by what we now do.*"

[9] *Nature* is put for *natural affection*, and *with merit* is used adverbially: "That I may extend my largest bounty where natural affection justly, or *meritoriously*, challenges it"; that is, *claims it as due.*—CROSBY.

Dearer than eye-sight, space, and liberty;
Beyond what can be valued, rich or rare;
No less than life, with grace, health, beauty, honour;
As much as child e'er loved, or father found;
A love that makes breath poor, and speech unable;
Beyond all manner of so much I love you.[11]

CORDELIA. [*Aside.*] What shall Cordelia do?
Love, and be silent.

KING LEAR. Of all these bounds, even from this line to this,
With shadowy forests and with champains rich'd,[12]
With plenteous rivers and wide-skirted meads,
We make thee lady:[13] to thine and Albany's issue
Be this perpetual.—What says our second daughter,
Our dearest Regan, wife to Cornwall? Speak.

REGAN. Sir,
I am made of the self[14] metal that my sister is,
And prize me at her worth. In my true heart
I find she names my very deed of love;
Only she comes too short: that I profess[15]
Myself an enemy to all other joys,
Which the most precious square of sense[16] possesses;
And find I am alone felicitate[17]
In your dear highness' love.

CORDELIA. [*Aside.*] Then poor Cordelia!
And yet not so; since, I am sure, my love's
More richer than my tongue.

KING LEAR. To thee and thine hereditary ever
Remain this ample third of our fair kingdom;
No less in space, validity,[18] and pleasure,
Than that conferr'd on Goneril.—Now, our joy,
Although the last, not least; to whose young love

---

[10] "My love is a matter so weighty that words cannot *express* or *sustain* it."

[11] Beyond all assignable quantity. "I love you so much that there is no possibility of telling how much."

[12] *Rich'd* for *enriched.*—*Champains* are *plains*; hence *fertile.*

[13] The *lord* of a thing is, strictly speaking, the *owner* of it. And *lady* is here used as the counterpart of *lord* in this sense. So that to make one the *lady* of a thing is to make her the *owner* or *possessor* of it.

[14] The Poet often uses *self* with the sense of *self-same.*

[15] "She comes short of me *in this*, that I profess," &c.

[16] By *square of sense* I understand *fulness of sensibility* or *capacity of joy.* So that the meaning seems to be, "Which the finest susceptibility of happiness is capable of." Some have stumbled at the word *square* here. But why not "*square* of sense" as well as *circle of the senses*? which would be a very intelligible expression.

[17] *Felicitate*, a shortened form of *felicitated*, is *fortunate* or *made happy.* The Poet has many preterites so shortened; as *consecrate*, *suffocate*, &c.

[18] *Validity* for *value* or *worth.* Repeatedly so.

The vines of France and milk of Burgundy
Strive to be interess'd;[19] what can you say to draw
A third more opulent than your sisters? Speak.
CORDELIA. Nothing, my lord.
KING LEAR. Nothing!
CORDELIA. Nothing.
KING LEAR. Nothing will come of nothing: speak again.
CORDELIA. Unhappy that I am, I cannot heave
My heart into my mouth:[20] I love your majesty
According to my bond;[21] nor more nor less.
KING LEAR. How, how, Cordelia! mend your speech a little,
Lest it may mar your fortunes.
CORDELIA. Good my lord,
You have begot me, bred me, loved me: I
Return those duties back as[22] are right fit,
Obey you, love you, and most honour you.
Why have my sisters husbands, if they say
They love you all? Haply, when I shall wed,
That lord whose hand must take my plight shall carry
Half my love with him, half my care and duty:
Sure, I shall never marry like my sisters,
To love my father all.
KING LEAR. But goes thy heart with this?
CORDELIA. Ay, good my lord.
KING LEAR. So young, and so untender?
CORDELIA. So young, my lord, and true.
KING LEAR. Let it be so; thy truth, then, be thy dower:
For, by the sacred radiance of the sun,
The mysteries of Hecate, and the night;
By all the operation of the orbs
From whom[23] we do exist, and cease to be;
Here I disclaim all my paternal care,
Propinquity and property of blood,
And as a stranger to my heart and me
Hold thee, from this, for ever. The barbarous Scythian,
Or he that makes his generation[24] messes

---

[19] To *interest* and to *interesse* are not, perhaps, different spellings of the same verb, but two distinct words, though of the same import; the one being derived from the Latin, the other from the French *interesser.*

[20] We have the same thought well expressed in *The Maid's Tragedy* of Beaumont and Fletcher, i. 1: "My mouth is much too narrow for my heart."

[21] *Bond* was used of any thing that *binds* or *obliges*; that is, *duty.*

[22] *As* is here a relative pronoun, referring to *those duties; which* or *that.* The word was used very loosely in the Poet's time.

[23] The relatives *who* and *which* were used indiscriminately.

[24] Probably meaning his *children;* perhaps simply his *kind.*

To gorge his appetite, shall to my bosom
Be as well neighbour'd, pitied, and relieved,
As thou my sometime[25] daughter.
KENT. Good my liege,—
KING LEAR. Peace, Kent!
Come not between the dragon and his wrath.
I loved her most, and thought to set my rest
On her kind nursery. Hence, and avoid my sight![26]
So be my grave my peace, as here I give
Her father's heart from her!—Call France; who stirs?
Call Burgundy.—Cornwall and Albany,
With my two daughters' dowers digest this third:
Let pride, which she calls plainness, marry her.
I do invest you jointly with my power,
Pre-eminence, and all the large effects
That troop with majesty. Ourself, by monthly course,
With reservation of an hundred knights,
By you to be sustain'd, shall our abode
Make with you by due turns. Only we still retain
The name, and all the additions to a King;[27]
The sway, revenue, execution of the rest,
Beloved sons, be yours: which to confirm,
This coronet part betwixt you. [*Giving the crown.*]
KENT. Royal Lear,
Whom I have ever honour'd as my King,
Loved as my father, as my master follow'd,
As my great patron thought on in my prayers,—
KING LEAR. The bow is bent and drawn, make from the shaft.
KENT. Let it fall rather, though the fork invade
The region of my heart: be Kent unmannerly,
When Lear is mad. What wilt thou do, old man?
Think'st thou that duty shall have dread to speak,
When power to flattery bows? To plainness honour's bound,
When majesty stoops to folly. Reverse thy doom;
And, in thy best consideration, cheque
This hideous rashness: answer my life my judgment,[28]
Thy youngest daughter does not love thee least;

---

[25] *Sometime*, here, is *former* or *formerly.*

[26] As Kent has said nothing to provoke this snappish order, we are probably to suppose that Lear, knowing his man, anticipates a bold remonstrance from him, and, in his excited mood, flares up at the thought of such a thing. So he says to him a little after, "Out of my sight."

[27] All the *titles* or *marks of honour* pertaining to *royalty.*

[28] "Let my life be answerable for my judgment," or, "I will stake my life on the truth of what I say."

Nor are those empty-hearted whose low sound
Reverbs[29] no hollowness.

KING LEAR. Kent, on thy life, no more.

KENT. My life I never held but as a pawn
To wage against thy enemies;[30] nor fear to lose it,
Thy safety being the motive.

KING LEAR. Out of my sight!

KENT. See better, Lear; and let me still remain
The true blank of thine eye.[31]

KING LEAR. Now, by Apollo,—

KENT. Now, by Apollo, King,
Thou swear'st thy gods in vain.

KING LEAR. [*Grasping his sword.*] O, vassal! miscreant!

ALBANY & CORNWALL. Dear sir, forbear.

KENT. Do;
Kill thy physician, and the fee bestow
Upon thy foul disease. Revoke thy doom;
Or, whilst I can vent clamour from my throat,
I'll tell thee thou dost evil.

KING LEAR. Hear me, recreant!
On thine allegiance, hear me!
Since thou hast sought to make us break our vow,—
Which we durst never yet,—and with strain'd pride
To come between our sentence and our power,—
Which nor our nature nor our place can bear,—
Our potency made good, take thy reward.[32]
Five days we do allot thee, for provision
To shield thee from diseases[33] of the world;
And on the sixth to turn thy hated back
Upon our kingdom: if, on the tenth day following,
Thy banish'd trunk be found in our dominions,
The moment is thy death. Away! by Jupiter,
This shall not be revoked.

KENT. Fare thee well, King: sith thus thou wilt appear,
Freedom lives hence, and banishment is here.—
[*to* CORDELIA.] The gods to their dear shelter take thee, maid,
That justly think'st, and hast most rightly said!—

---

[29] *Reverbs* for *reverberates*; probably a word of the Poet's own coining. Here it has the sense of *report* or *proclaim.*

[30] To *wage* is to *wager,* to *stake* or *hazard.* So, "I never held my life but as a thing to be impawned or put in pledge against your enemies."

[31] The *blank* is the *mark* at which men shoot. "See better," says Kent, "and let me be the mark to direct your sight, that you err not."

[32] That is, "Take thy reward *in* or *by a demonstration* of our power."

[33] *Disease* in its old sense of *discomfort* or what causes uneasiness.

[*to* REGAN *and* GONERIL.] And your large speeches may your
    deeds approve,[34]
That good effects may spring from words of love.
Thus Kent, O princes, bids you all adieu;
He'll shape his old course in a country new. [*Exit.*]

[*Flourish. Re-enter* GLOUCESTER, *with* KING OF FRANCE,
    BURGUNDY, *and* ATTENDANTS.]

GLOUCESTER. Here's France and Burgundy, my noble lord.
KING LEAR. My lord of Burgundy.
    We first address towards you, who with this King
    Hath rivall'd for our daughter: what, in the least,
    Will you require in present dower with her,
    Or cease your quest[35] of love?
BURGUNDY. Most royal majesty,
    I crave no more than what your highness offer'd,
    Nor will you tender less.
KING LEAR. Right noble Burgundy,
    When she was dear to us, we did hold her so;
    But now her price is fall'n. Sir, there she stands:
    If aught within that little seeming substance,
    Or all of it, with our displeasure pieced,[36]
    And nothing more, may fitly like your grace,
    She's there, and she is yours.
BURGUNDY. I know no answer.
KING LEAR. Will you, with those infirmities she owes,[37]
    Unfriended, new-adopted to our hate,
    Dower'd with our curse, and stranger'd with our oath,
    Take her, or leave her?
BURGUNDY. Pardon me, royal sir;
    Election makes not up on such conditions.
KING LEAR. Then leave her, sir; for, by the power that made me,
    I tell you all her wealth.—[*To* KING OF FRANCE.] For you, great
        King,
    I would not from your love make such a stray,
    To match[38] you where I hate; therefore beseech you

---

[34] *Approve* in the sense of *make good*, or *prove true*. Often so.

[35] A *quest* is a *seeking* or *pursuit*: the expedition in which a knight was engaged is often so named in *The Faerie Queene.*

[36] With our displeasure *added to it*; as in the common phrase of *piecing out* a thing.—*Like*, in the next line, was continually used where we should use *please. It likes me* is, in old language, the same as *I like it.*

[37] *Owes* and *owns* are but different forms of the same word.

[38] "Such a stray, *as* to match." So again in the next speech: "So monstrous, *as* to dismantle." The Poet omits *as* in such cases, when the verse is against it.

To avert your liking a more worthier way
Than on a wretch whom nature is ashamed
Almost to acknowledge hers.
KING OF FRANCE. This is most strange,
That she, that even but now was your best object,
The argument of your praise, balm of your age,
Most best, most dearest, should in this trice of time
Commit a thing so monstrous, to dismantle
So many folds of favour. Sure, her offence
Must be of such unnatural degree,
That monsters it, or your fore-vouch'd affection
Fall'n into taint;[39] which to believe of her,
Must be a faith that reason without miracle
Could never plant in me.
CORDELIA. I yet beseech your majesty,—
(If for I want[40] that glib and oily art,
To speak and purpose not; since what I well intend,
I'll do't before I speak,) that you make known
It is no vicious blot, murder, or foulness,
No unchaste action, or dishonour'd step,
That hath deprived me of your grace and favour;
But even for want of that for which I am richer,
A still-soliciting eye,[41] and such a tongue
As I am glad I have not, though not to have it
Hath lost me in your liking.
KING LEAR. Better thou
Hadst not been born than not t' have pleased me better.
KING OF FRANCE. Is it but this, a tardiness in nature
Which often leaves the history unspoke
That it intends to do?—My lord of Burgundy,
What say you to the lady? Love's not love
When it is mingled with regards[42] that stand
Aloof from the entire point. Will you have her?
She is herself a dowry.

---

[39] "*Must be* fall'n" is the meaning. *Taint* for *attaint* or *attainder*. "The affection which you before professed must have fallen under reproach or impeachment as fickle or false."—"Of *such* unnatural degree, *that monsters it*," is of such unnatural degree *as to be monstrous*, or *prove her a monster*.

[40] That is, "If it *be because* I want," or "If *you are doing this because* I want." The use of *for* in the sense of *because* is very frequent.

[41] "A *soliciting* eye" here means a *greedy, self-seeking, covetous* eye. The Poet often has *still* in the sense of *ever* or *continually*.—The preceding line will hardly bear a grammatical analysis, but the sense is plain enough. "The want of that for which" means, simply, "that want for which," or, if you please, "the want of that for the want of which."

[42] *Regards* for *considerations* or *inducements*. The same with *respects* in the fourth speech after. So the latter word is commonly used by the Poet.

BURGUNDY. Royal Lear,
    Give but that portion which yourself proposed,
    And here I take Cordelia by the hand,
    Duchess of Burgundy.
KING LEAR. Nothing: I have sworn; I am firm.
BURGUNDY. I am sorry, then, you have so lost a father
    That you must lose a husband.
CORDELIA. Peace be with Burgundy!
    Since that respects of fortune are his love,
    I shall not be his wife.
KING OF FRANCE. Fairest Cordelia, that art most rich, being poor;
    Most choice, forsaken; and most loved, despised!
    Thee and thy virtues here I seize upon:
    Be it lawful I take up what's cast away.—
    Gods, gods! 'tis strange that from their cold'st neglect
    My love should kindle to inflamed respect.—
    Thy dowerless daughter, King, thrown to my chance,
    Is queen of us, of ours, and our fair France:
    Not all the dukes of waterish[43] Burgundy
    Can buy this unprized precious maid of me.—
    Bid them farewell, Cordelia, though unkind:
    Thou losest here, a better where to find.
KING LEAR. Thou hast her, France: let her be thine; for we
    Have no such daughter, nor shall ever see
    That face of hers again.—Therefore be gone
    Without our grace, our love, our benison.[44]—
    Come, noble Burgundy.

    [*Flourish. Exeunt* KING LEAR, BURGUNDY, CORNWALL,
    ALBANY, GLOSTER, *and* ATTENDANTS.]

KING OF FRANCE. Bid farewell to your sisters.
CORDELIA. The jewels of our father, with wash'd eyes
    Cordelia leaves you: I know you what you are;
    And like a sister am most loath to call
    Your faults as they are named. Use well our father:
    To your professed[45] bosoms I commit him
    But yet, alas, stood I within his grace,
    I would prefer him to a better place.
    So, farewell to you both.

---

    [43] *Waterish* is here used with a dash of contempt. Burgundy, a level, well-watered country, was famous for its pastures and dairy-produce.
    [44] The Poet uses *benison* for *blessing*, when he wants a trisyllable.
    [45] *Professed* for *professing*; the passive form with the active sense. So in *Paradise Lost*, i. 486: "Likening his Maker to the *grazed* ox."

REGAN. Prescribe not us our duties.

GONERIL. Let your study
Be to content your lord, who hath received you
At fortune's alms. You have obedience scanted,
And well are worth the want that you have wanted.[46]

CORDELIA. Time shall unfold what plighted[47] cunning hides:
Who cover faults, at last shame them derides.
Well may you prosper!

KING OF FRANCE. Come, my fair Cordelia.

[*Exeunt* KING OF FRANCE *and* CORDELIA.]

GONERIL. Sister, it is not a little I have to say of what most nearly appertains to us both. I think our father will hence to-night.

REGAN. That's most certain, and with you; next month with us.

GONERIL. You see how full of changes his age is; the observation we have made of it hath not been little: he always loved our sister most; and with what poor judgment he hath now cast her off appears too grossly.

REGAN. 'Tis the infirmity of his age: yet he hath ever but slenderly known himself.

GONERIL. The best and soundest of his time hath been but rash; then must we look to receive from his age, not alone the imperfections of long-engrafted condition,[48] but therewithal the unruly waywardness that infirm and choleric years bring with them.

REGAN. Such unconstant starts are we like to have from him as this of Kent's banishment.

GONERIL. There is further compliment of leave-taking between France and him. Pray you, let's hit together:[49] if our father carry authority with such dispositions as he bears, this last surrender of his will but offend us.

REGAN. We shall further think on't.

GONERIL. We must do something, and i' the heat.[50] [*Exeunt.*]

---

[46] "You well deserve to want that in which you have been wanting."

[47] *Plight, pleat,* and *plait* are but different forms of the same word, all meaning to *fold, complicate,* and so *make dark.*

[48] Temper, or *disposition,* set and confirmed by long habit.

[49] "Let us *agree* or *unite* in the same plan or course of action."—The meaning of what follows probably is, "If the King continue in the same rash, headstrong, and inconstant temper as he has just shown in snatching back his authority the moment his will is crossed, we shall be the worse off for his surrender of the kingdom to us."

[50] So in the common phrase, "Strike while the iron's hot."

SCENE II.

A Hall in the EARL OF GLOUCESTER'*s Castle.*

[*Enter* EDMUND, *with a letter.*]

EDMUND. Thou, nature, art my goddess; to thy law
　　My services are bound.[51] Wherefore should I
　　Stand in the plague of custom, and permit
　　The curiosity of nations to deprive me,[52]
　　For that I am some twelve or fourteen moon-shines
　　Lag of a brother? Why bastard? wherefore base?
　　When my dimensions are as well compact,
　　My mind as generous, and my shape as true,
　　As honest madam's issue? Why brand they us
　　With base? with baseness? bastardy? base, base?
　　Who, in the lusty stealth of nature, take
　　More composition and fierce quality
　　Than doth, within a dull, stale, tired bed,
　　Go to the creating a whole tribe of fops,
　　Got 'tween asleep and wake?—Well, then,
　　Legitimate Edgar, I must have your land:
　　Our father's love is to the bastard Edmund
　　As to the legitimate: fine word,—*legitimate*!
　　Well, my legitimate, if this letter speed,
　　And my invention thrive, Edmund the base
　　Shall top th' legitimate.[53] I grow; I prosper:—
　　Now, gods, stand up for bastards!

[*Enter* GLOUCESTER.]

GLOUCESTER. Kent banish'd thus! and France in choler parted![54]
　　And the King gone to-night! subscribed his power!
　　Confined to exhibition! All this done

---

[51] In this speech of Edmund you see, as soon as a man cannot reconcile himself to reason, how his conscience flies off by way of appeal to Nature, who is sure upon such occasions never to find fault; and also how shame sharpens a predisposition in the heart to evil.—COLERIDGE.

[52] To "stand in the plague of custom" is, in Edmund's sense, to lie under the ban of conventional disability.—"The curiosity of nations" is the moral strictness of civil institutions; especially the law of marriage, and the exclusion of bastards from the rights of inheritance.—To *deprive* was sometimes used for to *cut off*, to *disinherit*. *Exheredo* is rendered by this word in the old dictionaries.

[53] To *top* is to *rise above*, to *surpass*. A frequent usage.

[54] *Parted* for *departed*. Also a frequent usage.

Upon the Gad![55]—Edmund, how now! what news?

EDMUND. So please your lordship, none.

[*Putting up the letter.*]

GLOUCESTER. Why so earnestly seek you to put up that letter?

EDMUND. I know no news, my lord.

GLOUCESTER. What paper were you reading?

EDMUND. Nothing, my lord.

GLOUCESTER. No? What needed, then, that terrible[56] dispatch of it into your pocket? the quality of nothing hath not such need to hide itself. Let's see: come, if it be nothing, I shall not need spectacles.

EDMUND. I beseech you, sir, pardon me: it is a letter from my brother, that I have not all o'er-read; and for so much as I have perused, I find it not fit for your o'er-looking.

GLOUCESTER. Give me the letter, sir.

EDMUND. I shall offend, either to detain or give it. The contents, as in part I understand them, are to blame.

GLOUCESTER. Let's see, let's see.

EDMUND. I hope, for my brother's justification, he wrote this but as an essay or taste of my virtue.

GLOUCESTER. [*Reads.*] *This policy and reverence of age*[57] *makes the world bitter to the best of our times; keeps our fortunes from us till our oldness cannot relish them. I begin to find an idle and fond*[58] *bondage in the oppression of aged tyranny; who sways, not as it hath power, but as it is suffered. Come to me, that of this I may speak more. If our father would sleep till I waked him, you should half his revenue for ever, and live the beloved of your brother,* EDGAR.

Hum—conspiracy!—*Sleep till I waked him,—you should enjoy half his revenue.*—My son Edgar! Had he a hand to write this? a heart and brain to breed it in?—When came this to you? who brought it?

---

[55] "*Subscribed* his power," is *yielded* or *given up* his power; as when we say a man has signed away his wealth, his freedom, or his rights.—"*Confined* to *exhibition*" is *limited* to an *allowance*. So in Ben Jonson's *Poetaster*: "Thou art a younger brother, and hast nothing but thy bare *exhibition*." The word is still so used in the English Universities.—*Upon the gad* is in haste; the same as *upon the star*. A *gad* was a sharp-pointed piece of steel, used in driving oxen; hence *goaded*.

[56] *Terrible* because done as if *from terror; terrified*.

[57] That is, this policy, or custom, *of reverencing age*. The idea is, that the honouring of fathers and mothers is an old superstition, which smart boys ought to cast off, knock their fathers on the head, and so have a good time while they are young. We have a like expression in scene4: "This milky *gentleness* and course of yours."

[58] Here, as commonly in Shakespeare, *fond* is *foolish*.

EDMUND. It was not brought me, my lord; there's the cunning of it; I found it thrown in at the casement of my closet.

GLOUCESTER. You know the character to be your brother's?

EDMUND. If the matter were good, my lord, I durst swear it were his; but, in respect of that, I would fain think it were not.

GLOUCESTER. It is his.

EDMUND. It is his hand, my lord; but I hope his heart is not in the contents.

GLOUCESTER. Hath he never heretofore sounded you in this business?

EDMUND. Never, my lord: but I have heard him oft maintain it to be fit, that, sons at perfect age, and fathers declining, the father should be as ward to the son, and the son manage his revenue.

GLOUCESTER. O villain, villain! His very opinion in the letter! Abhorred villain! Unnatural, detested,[59] brutish villain! worse than brutish!—Go, sirrah, seek him; I'll apprehend him: abominable villain! Where is he?

EDMUND. I do not well know, my lord. If it shall please you to suspend your indignation against my brother till you can derive from him better testimony of his intent, you shall run a certain course; where,[60] if you violently proceed against him, mistaking his purpose, it would make a great gap in your own honour, and shake in pieces the heart of his obedience. I dare pawn down my life for him, that he hath wrote this to feel my affection to your honour, and to no further pretence[61] of danger.

GLOUCESTER. Think you so?

EDMUND. If your honour judge it meet, I will place you where you shall hear us confer of this, and by an auricular assurance have your satisfaction; and that without any further delay than this very evening.

GLOUCESTER. He cannot be such a monster—

EDMUND. Nor is not, sure.

GLOUCESTER.—to his father, that so tenderly and entirely loves him.—Heaven and Earth!—Edmund, seek him out: wind me into him,[62] I pray you: frame the business after your own wisdom. I would unstate myself, to be in a due resolution.[63]

---

[59] *Detested* for *detestable.* The Poet so uses a good many words ending in *-ed.*

[60] *Where* and *whereas* were used indiscriminately.—Here, "a *certain* course" is a *safe* or *sure* course.

[61] *Pretence* was very often used for *intention* or *purpose.*

[62] *Me* is here *expletive.*—*Wind into him* is the same as our phrase "worm yourself into him"; that is, find out his hidden purpose.

[63] "I would give my whole estate, all that I possess, to be *satisfied* or *assured* in the matter." The Poet often has *resolve* in this sense.

EDMUND. I will seek him, sir, presently; convey[64] the business as I shall find means and acquaint you withal.

GLOUCESTER. These late eclipses in the sun and moon portend no good to us: though the wisdom of nature can reason it thus and thus, yet nature finds itself scourged by the sequent effects:[65] love cools, friendship falls off, brothers divide; in cities, mutinies; in countries, discord; in palaces, treason; and the bond cracked 'twixt son and father. This villain of mine comes under the prediction; there's son against father: the King falls from bias of nature; there's father against child. We have seen the best of our time: machinations, hollowness, treachery, and all ruinous disorders, follow us disquietly to our graves. Find out this villain, Edmund; it shall lose thee nothing; do it carefully. And the noble and true-hearted Kent banished! his offence, honesty! 'Tis strange. [*Exit.*]

EDMUND. This is the excellent foppery of the world, that, that, when we are sick in fortune,—often the surfeit of our own behavior,—we make guilty of our disasters the sun, the moon, and the stars: as if we were villains by necessity; fools by heavenly compulsion; knaves, thieves, and treachers,[66] by spherical predominance; drunkards, liars, and adulterers, by an enforced obedience of planetary influence; and all that we are evil in, by a divine thrusting on: an admirable evasion of whoremaster man, to lay his goatish disposition to the charge of a star![67] My father compounded with my mother under the dragon's tail; and my nativity was under Ursa major; so that it follows, I am rough and lecherous. Tut, I should have been that I am, had the maidenliest star in the firmament twinkled on my bastardizing. Edgar—

[*Enter* EDGAR.]

And pat he comes like the catastrophe of the old comedy.[68] My cue

---

[64] To *convey*, as the word is here used, is to *manage* or *carry through* a thing adroitly, or as by sleight of hand.

[65] "Though reason or natural philosophy may make out that these strange events proceed from the regular operation of natural laws, and so have no moral purpose or significance, yet we find them followed by calamities, as in punishment of our sins."

[66] *Treachers* for *traitors*. The word is used by Chaucer and Spenser.

[67] Warburton thinks that the dotages of judicial astrology were meant to be satirized in this speech. Coleridge remarks upon Edmund's philosophizing as follows: "Thus scorn and misanthropy are often the anticipations and mouthpieces of wisdom in the detection of superstitions. Both individuals and nations may be free from such prejudices by being below them, as well as by rising above them."

[68] Perhaps alluding, satirically, to the awkward catastrophes of the old comedies, which were coarsely contrived so as to have the persons enter, pat, just when they were wanted on the stage.—*Cue*, as here used, is *prompt-word* or *hint.*—*Bedlam*, an old corruption of *Bethlehem*, was a well-known hospital for the insane.—*Tom* was a name commonly given to Bedlamites. An instance of it will be seen afterwards in Edgar.—

is villainous melancholy, with a sigh like Tom o' Bedlam.—O,
these eclipses do portend these divisions! fa, sol, la, mi.[69]

EDGAR. How now, brother Edmund! what serious contemplation are
you in?

EDMUND. I am thinking, brother, of a prediction I read this other day,
what should follow these eclipses.

EDGAR. Do you busy yourself about that?

EDMUND. I promise you, the effects he writes of succeed unhappily:[70]
as of unnaturalness between the child and the parent; death, dearth,
dissolutions of ancient amities; divisions in state, menaces and
maledictions against King and nobles; needless diffidences,[71]
banishment of friends, dissipation of cohorts, nuptial breaches, and
I know not what.

EDGAR. How long have you been a sectary astronomical?[72]

EDMUND. Come, come; when saw you my father last?

EDGAR. Why, the night gone by.

EDMUND. Spake you with him?

EDGAR. Ay, two hours together.

EDMUND. Parted you in good terms? Found you no displeasure in him
by word or countenance?

EDGAR. None at all.

EDMUND. Bethink yourself wherein you may have offended him: and
at my entreaty forbear his presence till some little time hath
qualified the heat of his displeasure; which at this instant so rageth
in him, that with the mischief of your person it would scarcely
allay.

EDGAR. Some villain hath done me wrong.

EDMUND. That's my fear. I pray you, have a continent[73] forbearance
till the spied of his rage goes slower; and, as I say, retire with me
to my lodging, from whence I will fitly bring you to hear my lord
speak: pray ye, go; there's my key: if you do stir abroad, go armed.

EDGAR. Armed, brother!

Edmund is here pretending not to be aware of his brother's entrance.

[69] "Shakespeare shows by the context that he was well acquainted with the property
of these syllables in solmization, which imply a series of sounds so unnatural that ancient
musicians prohibited their use. Edmund, speaking of the eclipses as portents, compares
the dislocation of events, the *times being out of joint*, to the unnatural and offensive
sounds *fa sol la mi*." So says Dr. Burney. But Mr. Chappell, perhaps a better authority,
assures Mr. W. A. Wright, the Clarendon editor, that there is no foundation for Burney's
remark; and that "Edmund is merely singing to himself in order not to seem to observe
Edgar's approach."

[70] That is, *turn out badly*. The Poet often uses *success* for *issue* or *consequence*,
whether good or bad. The usage was common.

[71] *Diffidences* for *distrustings*, ruptures of confidence. An old usage.

[72] "How long have you belonged to the *sect of astronomers*?" Judicial astrology, as
it is called, formerly had its schools and professors.

[73] *Continent* in its old sense of *self-retrained* or *subdued*.

EDMUND. Brother, I advise you to the best; go armed: I am no honest
    man if there be any good meaning towards you: I have told you
    what I have seen and heard; but faintly,[74] nothing like the image
    and horror of it: pray you, away.
EDGAR. Shall I hear from you anon?
EDMUND. I do serve you in this business.—[*Exit* EDGAR.]
    A credulous father! and a brother noble,
    Whose nature is so far from doing harms,
    That he suspects none: on whose foolish honesty
    My practices[75] ride easy! I see the business.
    Let me, if not by birth, have lands by wit:
    All with me's meet that I can fashion fit. [*Exit.*]

SCENE III.

A Room in ALBANY's *Palace.*

[*Enter* GONERIL, *and* OSWALD.]

GONERIL. Did my father strike my gentleman for chiding of his Fool?
OSWALD. Yes, madam.
GONERIL. By day and night he wrongs me; every hour
    He flashes into one gross crime or other,
    That sets us all at odds: I'll not endure it:
    His knights grow riotous, and himself upbraids us
    On every trifle. When he returns from hunting,
    I will not speak with him; say I am sick:
    If you come slack of former services,
    You shall do well; the fault of it I'll answer. [*Horns within.*]
OSWALD. He's coming, madam; I hear him.
GONERIL. Put on what weary negligence you please,
    You and your fellows; I'll have it come to question:
    If he dislike it, let him to our sister,
    Whose mind and mine, I know, in that are one,
    Not to be over-ruled. Idle old man,
    That still would manage those authorities
    That he hath given away! Now, by my life,
    Old fools are babes again; and must be used
    With cheques as flatteries,—when they are seen abused.
    Remember what I tell you.
OSWALD. Well, madam.
GONERIL. And let his knights have colder looks among you;

---

[74] *Faintly* is *imperfectly,* and qualifies *told.*
[75] *Contrivance, plot, stratagem* are old meanings of *practice.*

What grows of it, no matter; advise your fellows so:
I would breed from hence occasions, and I shall,
That I may speak: I'll write straight to my sister,
To hold my very course. Prepare for dinner. [*Exeunt.*]

SCENE IV.

A Hall in the Same.

[*Enter* KENT, *disguised.*]

KENT. If but as well I other accents borrow,
That can my speech defuse,[76] my good intent
May carry through itself to that full issue
For which I razed my likeness. Now, banish'd Kent,
If thou canst serve where thou dost stand condemn'd,—
So may it come!—thy master, whom thou lovest,
Shall find thee full of labours.

[*Horns within. Enter* KING LEAR, KNIGHTS, *and*
ATTENDANTS.]

KING LEAR. Let me not stay a jot for dinner; go get it ready.
    [*Exit an* ATTENDANT.]—How now! what art thou?
KENT. A man, sir.
KING LEAR. What dost thou profess? what wouldst thou with us?
KENT. I do profess to be no less than I seem; to serve him truly that
    will put me in trust: to love him that is honest; to converse[77] with
    him that is wise, and says little; to fear judgment; to fight when I
    cannot choose; and to eat no fish.[78]
KING LEAR. What art thou?
KENT. A very honest-hearted fellow, and as poor as the King.
KING LEAR. If thou be as poor for a subject as he is for a King, thou
    art poor enough. What wouldst thou?

---

[76] To *defuse* (sometimes spelt *diffuse*) is to *confuse*, and to *disguise* by confusing;
though the general sense of *disorder* seems to lie at the bottom of the word. It appears
that the form *defuse* was common in the Poet's time. So in Armin's *Nest of Ninnies*: "It is
hard that the taste of one apple should distaste the whole lumpe of this *defused* chaios."—
Kent has disguised his person so as to pass unrecognized; and now he is apprehensive
that his speech or accents may betray him.

[77] To *converse* signifies properly to *keep company*, to have *commerce* with. His
meaning is, that he chooses for his companions men who are not tattlers or talebearers.

[78] *Eating fish* on the fast-days of the Church, though enjoined by the civil
authorities, was odious to the more advanced Protestants as a badge of popery. So in
Marston's *Dutch Courtezan*: "I trust I am none of *the wicked* that *eat fish* a fridays." This
is probably the reason why Kent makes eating no fish a recommendation to employment.

KENT. Service.

KING LEAR. Who wouldst thou serve?

KENT. You.

KING LEAR. Dost thou know me, fellow?

KENT. No, sir; but you have that in your countenance which I would fain call master.

KING LEAR. What's that?

KENT. Authority.

KING LEAR. What services canst thou do?

KENT. I can keep honest counsel, ride, run, mar a curious tale in telling it, and deliver a plain message bluntly: that which ordinary men are fit for, I am qualified in; and the best of me is diligence.

KING LEAR. How old art thou?

KENT. Not so young, sir, to love a woman for singing, nor so old to dote on her for any thing: I have years on my back forty eight.

KING LEAR. Follow me; thou shalt serve me: if I like thee no worse after dinner, I will not part from thee yet.—Dinner, ho, dinner!—Where's my knave?[79] my Fool?—Go you, and call my Fool hither.—[*Exit an* ATTENDANT.]

[*Enter* OSWALD.]

You, you, sirrah, where's my daughter?

OSWALD. So please you,—[*Exit.*]

KING LEAR. What says the fellow there? Call the clotpoll[80] back. [*Exit a* KNIGHT.]—Where's my Fool, ho? I think the world's asleep.—

[*Re-enter* KNIGHT.]

How now! where's that mongrel?

KNIGHT. He says, my lord, your daughter is not well.

KING LEAR. Why came not the slave back to me when I called him.

KNIGHT. Sir, he answered me in the roundest[81] manner, he would not.

KING LEAR. He would not!

KNIGHT. My lord, I know not what the matter is; but, to my judgment, your highness is not entertained with that ceremonious affection as you were wont; there's a great abatement of kindness appears as well in the general dependants as in the duke himself also and your daughter.

---

[79] *Knave* was a common term of familiar endearment.

[80] *Clot* is *clod*, and *poll* is *head*; so that *clotpoll* comes to *blockhead*.

[81] *Round* is *blunt, downright, plain-spoken*.

KING LEAR. Ha! sayest thou so?

KNIGHT. I beseech you, pardon me, my lord, if I be mistaken; for my
duty cannot be silent when I think your highness wronged.

KING LEAR. Thou but rememberest me of mine own conception: I
have perceived a most faint neglect of late; which I have rather
blamed as mine own jealous curiosity than as a very pretence[82] and
purpose of unkindness: I will look further into't. But where's my
Fool? I have not seen him this two days.

KNIGHT. Since my young lady's going into France, sir, the Fool hath
much pined away.[83]

KING LEAR. No more of that; I have noted it well.—Go you, and tell
my daughter I would speak with her. [*Exit an* ATTENDANT.]—
Go you, call hither my Fool.—[*Exit an* ATTENDANT.]

[*Re-enter* OSWALD.]

O, you sir, you, come you hither, sir: who am I, sir?

OSWALD. My lady's father.

KING LEAR. *My lady's father*! my lord's knave: your whoreson dog!
you slave! you cur!

OSWALD. I am none of these, my lord; I beseech your pardon.

KING LEAR. Do you bandy looks with me, you rascal?

[*Striking him.*]

OSWALD. I'll not be struck, my lord.

KENT. Nor tripped neither, you base football player.

[*Tripping up his heels.*]

KING LEAR. I thank thee, fellow; thou servest me, and I'll love thee.

KENT. Come, sir, arise, away! I'll teach you differences: away, away!
if you will measure your lubber's length again, tarry: but away! go
to; have you wisdom? so.

---

[82] "Jealous curiosity" seems to mean a suspicious, prying scrutiny, on the watch to
detect slights and neglects.—*Pretence*, again, for *intent* or *design*—*Very* in the sense of
real or *deliberate*.—The passage is rather curious as discovering a sort of double
consciousness in the old King.

[83] This aptly touches the keynote of the Fool's character. "The Fool," says
Coleridge, "is no comic buffoon to make the groundlings laugh,—no forced
condescension of Shakespeare's genius to the taste of his audience. Accordingly the Poet
prepares for his introduction, which he never does with any of his common clowns and
Fools, by bringing him into living connection with the pathos of the play. He is as
wonderful a creation as Caliban: his wild babblings and inspired idiocy articulate and
gauge the horrors of the scene."

[*Pushes* OSWALD *out.*]

KING LEAR. Now, my friendly knave, I thank thee: there's earnest of thy service.

[*Giving* KENT *money.*]

[*Enter* FOOL.]

FOOL. Let me hire him too.—Here's my coxcomb.[84]

[*Offering* KENT *his cap.*]

KING LEAR. How now, my pretty knave! how dost thou?
FOOL. Sirrah, you were best take my coxcomb.
KENT. Why, Fool?
FOOL. Why, for taking one's part that's out of favour: nay, an thou canst not smile as the wind sits,[85] thou'lt catch cold shortly: there, take my coxcomb: why, this fellow has banished two on's daughters, and did the third a blessing against his will; if thou follow him, thou must needs wear my coxcomb.—How now, nuncle![86] Would I had two coxcombs and two daughters!
KING LEAR. Why, my boy?
FOOL. If I gave them all my living, I'd keep my coxcombs myself. There's mine; beg another of thy daughters.
KING LEAR. Take heed, sirrah; the whip.
FOOL. Truth's a dog must to kennel; he must be whipped out, when Lady, the brach,[87] may stand by the fire and stink.
KING LEAR. A pestilent gall to me!
FOOL. Sirrah, I'll teach thee a speech.
KING LEAR. Do.
FOOL. Mark it, nuncle:

---

[84] A *coxcomb* was one of the badges of an "allowed Fool." It was a cap with a piece of red cloth sewn upon the top, to resemble the comb of a cock.

[85] To "smile as the wind sits" is to fall in with and humour the disposition of those in power, or to curry favour with those who have rewards to bestow. The Fool means that Kent has earned the name of fool by not doing this, and should wear the appropriate badge.

[86] A familiar contraction of *mine uncle*. It seems that the common appellation of the old licensed Fool to his superiors was *uncle*. In Beaumont and Fletcher's *Pilgrim*, when Alinda assumes the character of a Fool, she uses the same language. She meets Alfonso, and calls him *nuncle*; to which he replies by calling her *naunt*.

[87] It appears that *brach* was a general term for a keen-scented hound. *Lady* is here the name of a female hound.

> Have more than thou showest,
> Speak less than thou knowest,
> Lend less than thou owest,[88]
> Ride more than thou goest,
> Learn more than thou trowest,[89]
> Set less than thou throwest;
> Leave thy drink and thy whore,
> And keep in-a-door,
> And thou shalt have more
> Than two tens to a score.

KENT. This is nothing, Fool.

FOOL. Then 'tis like the breath[90] of an unfee'd lawyer; you gave me nothing for't.—Can you make no use of nothing, nuncle?

KING LEAR. Why, no, boy; nothing can be made out of nothing.

FOOL. [*To* KENT.] Prithee, tell him, so much the rent of his land comes to: he will not believe a Fool.

KING LEAR. A bitter Fool!

FOOL. Dost thou know the difference, my boy, between a bitter Fool and a sweet Fool?

KING LEAR. No, lad; teach me.

FOOL.

> That lord that counsell'd thee
>   To give away thy land,
> Come place him here by me,
>   Or do thou for him stand:
> The sweet and bitter Fool
>   Will presently appear;
> The one in motley here,
>   The other found out there.

KING LEAR. Dost thou call me Fool, boy?

FOOL. All thy other titles thou hast given away; that thou wast born with.

KENT. This is not altogether Fool, my lord.

FOOL. No, faith, lords and great men will not let me; if I had a monopoly out, they would have part on't: and ladies too, they will not let me have all Fool to myself; they'll be snatching.—Give me

---

[88] That is, do not lend all that thou hast: *owe* for *own.*

[89] To *trow* is to *know.*—*Set,* in the next line, means *stake*: stake less than the value of what you throw *for.*

[90] *Breath* is here used for that in which a lawyer's breath is sometimes spent,—*words.*

an egg, nuncle, and I'll give thee two crowns.

KING LEAR. What two crowns shall they be?

FOOL. Why, after I have cut the egg i' the middle, and eat up the meat, the two crowns of the egg. When thou clovest thy crown i' the middle, and gavest away both parts, thou borest thy ass on thy back o'er the dirt:[91] thou hadst little wit in thy bald crown, when thou gavest thy golden one away. If I speak like myself in this, let him be whipped that first finds it so.[92]

[*Sings.*]

Fools had ne'er less wit in a year;
For wise men are grown foppish,
They know not how their wits to wear,
Their manners are so apish.[93]

KING LEAR. When were you wont to be so full of songs, sirrah?

FOOL. I have used it, nuncle, ever since thou madest thy daughters thy mothers: for when thou gavest them the rod, and put'st down thine own breeches,

[*Sings.*]

Then they for sudden joy did weep,
And I for sorrow sung,
That such a King should play bo-peep,
And go the fools among.

Prithee, nuncle, keep a schoolmaster that can teach thy Fool to lie: I would fain learn to lie.

KING LEAR. An you lie, sirrah, we'll have you whipped.

FOOL. I marvel what kin thou and thy daughters are: they'll have me whipped for speaking true, thou'lt have me whipped for lying; and sometimes I am whipped for holding my peace. I had rather be any kind o' thing than a Fool: and yet I would not be thee, nuncle; thou hast pared thy wit o' both sides, and left nothing i' the middle: here comes one o' the parings.

---

[91] Alluding, no doubt, to the fable of the old man and his ass.

[92] That is, "If in this I speak like a fool or foolishly, let not me be whipped for saying it, but let him have the whipping who first finds it to be as I have said." The sage Fool is darkly forecasting the troubles that await the old King as the consequences of what he has done. Fools were liable to be whipped for using too great freedom in sarcastic speech.

[93] "There never was a time when fools were less in favour; and this is because they were never so little wanted, for wise men supply their place."

[*Enter* GONERIL.]

KING LEAR. How now, daughter! what makes that frontlet[94] on?
 Methinks you are too much of late i' the frown.
FOOL. Thou wast a pretty fellow when thou hadst no need to care for
 her frowning; now thou art an O without a figure: I am better than
 thou art now; I am a Fool, thou art nothing.—[*To* GONERIL.] Yes,
 forsooth, I will hold my tongue; so your face bids me, though you
 say nothing. Mum, mum,

> *He that keeps nor crust nor crum,*
> *Weary of all, shall want some.*

That's a shealed peascod.[95] [*Pointing to* KING LEAR.]
GONERIL. Not only, sir, this your all-licensed Fool,
 But other of your insolent retinue
 Do hourly carp and quarrel; breaking forth
 In rank and not-to-be endured riots. Sir,
 I had thought, by making this well known unto you,
 To have found a safe redress; but now grow fearful,
 By what yourself too late have spoke and done.
 That you protect this course, and put it on
 By your allowance;[96] which if you should, the fault
 Would not 'scape censure, nor the redresses sleep,
 Which, in the tender of a wholesome weal,[97]
 Might in their working do you that offence,
 Which else were shame, that then necessity
 Will call discreet proceeding.
FOOL. For, you know, nuncle,

> *The hedge-sparrow fed the cuckoo so long,*
> *That it's had it head bit off by it young.*[98]

---

[94] "What *means* that *frown* on your brow?" or, "What business has it there?" The
verb to *make* was often used thus. A *frontlet* is said to have been a cloth worn on the
forehead by ladies to prevent wrinkles. Of course Goneril enters with a *cloud of anger* in
her face. So in *Zepheria*, 1594: "And vayle thy face with *frownes* as with a *frontlet*."

[95] Now a mere husk that contains nothing. *Cod*, or *peascod*, is the old name of what
we call *pod*, or *peapod*.

[96] To "*put* it *on* by your *allowance*" is to *encourage* it by your *approval*. *Put on* for
incite or *set on* was very common. Also *allow* and its derivatives in the sense of *approve*.

[97] "The tender of a wholesome weal" is the taking care that the commonwealth be
kept in a sound and healthy state. To *tender* a thing is to *be careful* of it.—*Wholesome* is
here used proleptically.

[98] Alluding to a trick which the cuckoo has of laying her eggs in the sparrow's nest,
to be hatched, and the cuckoo's chicks fed by the sparrow, till they get so big and so
voracious as to scare away or kill their feeder.

So, out went the candle, and we were left darkling.[99]

KING LEAR. Are you our daughter?

GONERIL. Come, sir,
I would you would make use of that good wisdom,
Whereof I know you are fraught; and put away
These dispositions, that of late transform you
From what you rightly are.

FOOL. May not an ass know when the cart draws the horse? *Whoop,
Jug! I love thee.*[100]

KING LEAR. Doth any here know me? This is not Lear: doth Lear
walk thus? speak thus? Where are his eyes? Either his notion
weakens, his discernings are lethargied.[101] Ha! waking? 'tis not so.
Who is it that can tell me who I am?—

FOOL. Lear's shadow,—

KING LEAR.—I would learn that; for, by the marks of sovereignty,
knowledge, and reason,—I should be false persuaded I had
daughters.[102]

FOOL.—which they will make an obedient father.[103]

KING LEAR. Your name, fair gentlewoman?

GONERIL. This admiration,[104] sir, is much o' the savour
Of other your new pranks. I do beseech you
To understand my purposes aright:
As you are old and reverend, you should be wise.
Here do you keep a hundred knights and squires;
Men so disorder'd, so debosh'd and bold,
That this our court, infected with their manners,

---

[99] To be left *darkling* is to be left in the dark.

[100] This is said to be a part of the burden of an old song. Halliwell notes upon it as follows: "*Jug* was the old nickname for *Joan*, and it was also a term of endearment. Edward Alleyn, the player, writing to his wife in 1593, says, 'And, Jug, I pray you, lett my orayng-tawny stokins of wolen be dyed a new good blak against I com hom, to wear in winter.'" He also quotes from Cotgrave's *Wit's Interpreter*, 1617: "If I be I, and thou be'st one, tell me, sweet Jugge, how spell'st thou Jone." And Heywood's *Rape of Lucrece*, 1638, as quoted by Furness, has a song which begins, "Arise, arise, my Juggie, my Puggie," and Juggie replies, "Begon, begon, my Willie, my Billie."

[101] *Notion* and *discernings* are evidently meant here as equivalent terms. *Notion* for *mind, judgment,* or *understanding,* occurs repeatedly. So that the meaning is, "Either his mind is breaking down, or else it has fallen into a lethargy."

[102] Here "marks of *sovereignty*," as I take it, are *sovereign* marks, and *knowledge* and *reason* in apposition with *marks*. So that the meaning is, "For knowledge and reason, which are our supreme guides or attributes, would persuade me I had daughters, though such is clearly not the case."

[103] It must be understood, that in the speech beginning "I would learn that," Lear is continuing his former speech, and answering his own question, without heeding the Fool's interruption. So, again, in this speech the Fool continues his former one, *which* referring to *shadow*.

[104] *Admiration* in its Latin sense of *wonder*.

Shows like a riotous inn: Epicurism and lust
Make it more like a tavern or a brothel
Than a graced palace. The shame itself doth speak
For instant remedy: be then desired
By her, that else will take the thing she begs,
A little to disquantity your train;
And the remainder, that shall still depend,
To be such men as may besort your age,
And know themselves and you.
KING LEAR. Darkness and devils!—
Saddle my horses; call my train together.—
Degenerate bastard! I'll not trouble thee:
Yet have I left a daughter.
GONERIL. You strike my people; and your disorder'd rabble
Make servants of their betters.

[*Enter* ALBANY.]

KING LEAR. Woe, that too late repents,—[*To* ALBANY.] O, sir, are
     you come?
Is it your will? Speak, sir.—Prepare my horses.—
Ingratitude, thou marble-hearted fiend,
More hideous when thou show'st thee in a child
Than the sea-monster![105]
ALBANY. Pray, sir, be patient.
KING LEAR. [*To* GONERIL.] Detested kite! thou liest.
My train are men of choice and rarest[106] parts,
That all particulars of duty know,
And in the most exact regard support
The worship[107] of their name.—O most small fault,
How ugly didst thou in Cordelia show!
That, like an engine,[108] wrench'd my frame of nature
From the fix'd place; drew from heart all love,
And added to the gall. O Lear, Lear, Lear!
Beat at this gate, that let thy folly in, [*Striking his head.*]
And thy dear judgment out!—Go, go, my people.
ALBANY. My lord, I am guiltless, as I am ignorant
Of what hath moved you.

---

[105] Referring, probably, to the dreadful beast that made such havoc with the virgin daughters of old Troy.
[106] Here the superlative sense in *rarest* extends back over *choice*. The usage was common.
[107] *Worship* was continually used just as *honour* is now, only meaning less. So "your *Worship*" was a lower title than "your *Honour*."
[108] *Engine* for *rack*, the old instrument of torture.

KING LEAR. It may be so, my lord.—Hear, nature, hear!
 Dear goddess, hear! suspend thy purpose, if
 Thou didst intend To make this creature fruitful:
 Into her womb convey sterility!
 Dry up in her the organs of increase;
 And from her derogate body never spring
 A babe to honour her! If she must teem,
 Create her child of spleen; that it may live,
 And be a thwart disnatured torment to her!
 Let it stamp wrinkles in her brow of youth;
 With cadent tears fret channels in her cheeks;
 Turn all her mother's pains and benefits
 To laughter and contempt; that she may feel
 How sharper than a serpent's tooth it is
 To have a thankless child!—Away, away! [*Exit.*]
ALBANY. Now, gods that we adore, whereof comes this?
GONERIL. Never afflict yourself to know the cause;
 But let his disposition have that scope
 That dotage gives it.

 [*Re-enter* KING LEAR.]

KING LEAR. What, fifty of my followers at a clap!
 Within a fortnight!
ALBANY. What's the matter, sir?
KING LEAR. I'll tell thee.—[*To* GONERIL.] Life and death! I am
  ashamed
 That thou hast power to shake my manhood thus;
 That these hot tears, which break from me perforce,
 Should make thee worth them. Blasts and fogs upon thee!
 The untented woundings[109] of a father's curse
 Pierce every sense about thee!—Old fond eyes,
 Beweep this cause again, I'll pluck ye out,
 And cast you, with the waters that you loose,
 To temper clay. Yea, it is come to this?
 Let it be so: yet have I left a daughter,
 Who, I am sure, is kind and comfortable:[110]
 When she shall hear this of thee, with her nails
 She'll flay thy wolvish visage. Thou shalt find
 That I'll resume the shape which thou dost think
 I have cast off for ever: thou shalt, I warrant thee.

---

[109] The *untented* woundings are the *rankling* or *never-healing wounds* inflicted by parental malediction. To *tent* is to *probe*: *untented*, therefore, is *too deep to be probed*; *incurable*. See page 32, note 59.

[110] *Comfortable* in the sense of *comforting* or *giving* comfort.

[*Exeunt* KING LEAR, KENT, *and* ATTENDANTS.]

GONERIL. Do you mark that, my lord?[111]
ALBANY. I cannot be so partial, Goneril,
    To the great love I bear you,—
GONERIL. Pray you, content.—What, Oswald, ho!—
    [*To the* FOOL.] You, sir, more knave than Fool, after your master.
FOOL. Nuncle Lear, nuncle Lear, tarry and take the Fool with thee.—

        A fox, when one has caught her,
        And such a daughter,
        Should sure to the slaughter,
        If my cap would buy a halter:
        So the Fool follows after. [*Exit.*]

GONERIL. This man hath had good counsel:—a hundred knights!
    'Tis politic and safe to let him keep
    At point[112] a hundred knights: yes, that, on every dream,
    Each buzz, each fancy, each complaint, dislike,
    He may enguard his dotage with their powers,
    And hold our lives in mercy.—Oswald, I say!—
ALBANY. Well, you may fear too far.[113]
GONERIL. Safer than trust too far:
    Let me still take away the harms I fear,
    Not fear still to be taken: I know his heart.
    What he hath utter'd I have writ my sister
    If she sustain him and his hundred knights
    When I have show'd the unfitness,—

    [*Re-enter* OSWALD.]

        How now, Oswald!
    What, have you writ that letter to my sister?
OSWALD. Yes, madam.
GONERIL. Take you some company, and away to horse:
    Inform her full of my particular fear;

---

    [111] Albany, though his heart is on the King's side, is reluctant to make a square issue with his wife; and she thinks to work upon him by calling his attention pointedly to Lear's threat of resuming the kingdom.

    [112] *At point* is *completely armed*, and so ready on the slightest notice.

    [113] The monster Goneril prepares what is necessary, while the character of Albany renders a still more maddening grievance possible, namely, Regan and Cornwall in perfect sympathy of monstrosity. Not a sentiment, not an image, which can give pleasure on its own account, is admitted: whenever these creatures are introduced, and they are brought forward as little as possible, pure horror reigns throughout.—COLERIDGE.

And thereto add such reasons of your own
As may compact it more.[114] Get you gone;
And hasten your return. [*Exit* OSWALD.]—No, no, my lord,
This milky gentleness and course[115] of yours
Though I condemn not, yet, under pardon,
You are much more attask'd[116] for want of wisdom
Than praised for harmful mildness.[117]

ALBANY. How far your eyes may pierce I can not tell:
Striving to better, oft we mar what's well.

GONERIL. Nay, then—

ALBANY. Well, well; the event.[118] [*Exeunt.*]

SCENE V.

Court before the Same.

[*Enter* KING LEAR, KENT, *and the* FOOL.]

KING LEAR. Go you before to Gloucester with these letters. Acquaint my daughter no further with any thing you know than comes from her demand out of the letter.[119] If your diligence be not speedy, I shall be there[120] afore you.

KENT. I will not sleep, my lord, till I have delivered your letter. [*Exit.*]

FOOL. If a man's brains were in's heels, were't not in danger of kibes?[121]

KING LEAR. Ay, boy.

FOOL. Then, I prithee, be merry; thy wit shall ne'er go slip-shod.[122]

---

[114] That is, make it more consistent and credible: *strengthen* it.

[115] "Milky and *gentle* course" is the meaning. See page 31, note 57.

[116] The word *task* is frequently used by Shakespeare and his contemporaries in the sense of *tax*. So in the common phrase of our time, "Taken to task"; that is, *called to account*, or *reproved*.

[117] That is, praised for a mildness that is harmful in its effects.

[118] As before implied, Albany shrinks from a word-storm with his helpmate, and so tells her, in effect, "Well, let us not quarrel about it, but wait and see how your course works." In their marriage, Goneril had somewhat the advantage of her husband; because, to be sure, she was a king's daughter, and he was not.

[119] This instruction to Kent is very well-judged. The old King feels mortified at what has happened, and does not want Kent to volunteer any information about it to his other daughter.

[120] The word *there* shows that when the King says, "Go you before to *Gloster*," he means the town of Gloster, which Shakespeare chose to make the residence of the Duke of Cornwall, to increase the probability of his setting out late from thence on a visit to the Earl of Gloster. The old English earls usually resided in the counties from whence they took their titles. Lear, not finding his son-in-law and daughter at home, follows them to the Earl of Gloster's castle.

[121] *Kibe* is an old name for a heel-sore.

[122] I do not well see the force or application of this. The best comment I have met

KING LEAR. Ha, ha, ha!

FOOL. Shalt see thy other daughter will use thee kindly;[123] for though she's as like this as a crab's[124] like an apple, yet I can tell what I can tell.

KING LEAR. Why, what canst thou tell, my boy?

FOOL. She will taste as like this as a crab does to a crab. Thou canst tell why one's nose stands i' the middle on's face?

KING LEAR. No.

FOOL. Why, to keep one's eyes of[125] either side's nose; that what a man cannot smell out, he may spy into.

KING LEAR. I did her wrong.[126]

FOOL. Canst tell how an oyster makes his shell?

KING LEAR. No.

FOOL. Nor I neither; but I can tell why a snail has a house.

KING LEAR. Why?

FOOL. Why, to put his head in; not to give it away to his daughters, and leave his horns without a case.

KING LEAR. I will forget my nature.[127] So kind a father!—Be my horses ready?

FOOL. Thy asses are gone about 'em. The reason why the seven stars[128] are no more than seven is a pretty reason.

KING LEAR. Because they are not eight?

FOOL. Yes, indeed: thou wouldst make a good Fool.

KING LEAR. To take't again perforce![129] Monster ingratitude!

FOOL. If thou wert my Fool, nuncle, I'd have thee beaten for being old before thy time.

KING LEAR. How's that?

---

with on the passage is Moberly's: "The Fool laughs at Kent's promise of rapidity, and says, first, that, 'when men's brains are in their heels,' (that is, when they have no more wit than is needed, to go fast,) 'they may get brain-chilblains'; and, secondly, that, 'as Lear has no brains, he is in no such danger.'"

[123] The Fool quibbles, using *kindly* in two senses; as it means *affectionately*, and like the rest of her *kind*, or according to her *nature*. The Poet often uses *kind* in this sense.

[124] *Crab* refers to the fruit so-called, not to the fish. So in Lyly's *Euphues*: The sower Crabbe hath the shew of an Apple as well as the sweet Pippin."

[125] Shakespeare often has *of* where we should use *on*, and *vice versa*; as *on's* in the Fool's preceding speech.

[126] Lear is now stung with remorse for his treatment of Cordelia.

[127] *Forget* in the sense of *put off*, *disown*, or *forsake*. Lear means that he will renounce the kindness which is naturally his.

[128] This is commonly thought to mean the constellation Pleiades. But I am apt to think that Mr. Furness is right: "May it not refer to 'the Great Bear, whose seven stars are the most conspicuous group in the circle of perpetual apparition in the Northern Hemisphere?—so conspicuous, indeed, that the Latin word for *North* was derived from them. We call this constellation 'The Dipper,' from its fancied resemblance to the utensil of that name; a name, I believe, scarcely known in England.

[129] He is meditating on what he has before threatened, namely, to "resume the shape which he has cast off."

FOOL. Thou shouldst not have been old till thou hadst been wise.
KING LEAR. O, let me not be mad,[130] not mad, sweet Heaven
Keep me in temper: I would not be mad!—

[*Enter a* GENTLEMAN.]

How now! are the horses ready?
GENTLEMAN. Ready, my lord.
KING LEAR. Come, boy.
FOOL. She that's a maid now, and laughs at my departure,
Shall not be a maid long, unless things be cut shorter. [*Exeunt.*]

ACT II.

SCENE I.

A Court within GLOUCESTER's *Castle.*

[*Enter* EDMUND, *and* CURAN *meeting.*]

EDMUND. Save thee, Curan.
CURAN. And you, sir. I have been with your father, and given him
notice that the Duke of Cornwall and Regan his duchess will be
here with him this night.
EDMUND. How comes that?
CURAN. Nay, I know not. You have heard of the news abroad; I mean
the whispered ones, for they are yet but ear-kissing arguments.[131]
EDMUND. Not I pray you, what are they?
CURAN. Have you heard of no likely wars toward[132] 'twixt the Dukes
of Cornwall and Albany?
EDMUND. Not a word.
CURAN. You may do, then, in time. Fare you well, sir. [*Exit.*]
EDMUND. The duke be here to-night? The better! best!
This weaves itself perforce into my business.
My father hath set guard to take my brother;
And I have one thing, of a queasy question,[133]
Which I must act: briefness and fortune, work!
Brother, a word; descend: brother, I say!

---

[130] The mind's own anticipation of madness! The deepest tragic notes are often
struck by a half-sense of the impending blow.—COLERIDGE.
[131] "*Ear-kissing* arguments" are words spoken with the speaker's lips close to the
hearer's ear, as if kissing him; *whispers.*
[132] *Toward* is *forthcoming* or *at hand.*
[133] "A *queasy* question" is a matter delicate, ticklish, or difficult to manage; as a
queasy stomach is impatient of motion.

[*Enter* EDGAR.]

My father watches: O sir, fly this place;
Intelligence is given where you are hid;
You have now the good advantage of the night:
Have you not spoken 'gainst the Duke of Cornwall?
He's coming hither: now, i' the night, i' the haste,
And Regan with him: have you nothing said
Upon his party 'gainst the Duke of Albany?
Advise yourself.[134]

EDGAR. I am sure on't, not a word.
EDMUND. I hear my father coming: pardon me:
     In cunning I must draw my sword upon you
     Draw; seem to defend yourself; now quit you[135] well.
     Yield: come before my father.—Light, ho, here!—
     Fly, brother.—Torches, torches!—So, farewell.—

[*Exit* EDGAR.]

Some blood drawn on me would beget opinion. [*Wounds his arm.*]
Of my more fierce endeavour: I have seen drunkards
Do more than this in sport.[136]—Father, father!—
Stop, stop!—No help?

[*Enter* GLOUCESTER, *and Servants with Torches.*]

GLOUCESTER. Now, Edmund, where's the villain?
EDMUND. Here stood he in the dark, his sharp sword out,
     Mumbling of wicked charms, conjuring the moon
     To stand auspicious mistress.[137]
GLOUCESTER. But where is he?

---

[134] That is, *bethink* yourself; question your memory; recollect.—The preceding line is commonly explained, "Have you said nothing *in* censure of the party he has formed against the Duke of Albany?" This supposes Edmund to be merely repeating the question he has asked before. But the proper sense of "upon his *party*" is "upon his *side*," or in his favour. So that Delius probably gives the right explanation. I quote from Furness's *Variorum*: "In order to confuse his brother, and urge him to a more speedy flight, by giving him the idea that he is surfounded by perils, Edmund asks Edgar, first, whether he has not spoken 'gainst the Duke of Cornwall, and then, reversing the question, asks whether he has not said something on the side of Cornwall 'gainst the Duke of Albany."

[135] *Quit you* is *acquit yourself.* The Poet has *quit* repeatedly so.

[136] These drunken feats are mentioned in Marston's *Dutch Courtezan*: "Have I not been drunk for your health, eat glasses, drunk wine *stabbed arms*, and done all offices of protested gallantry for your sake?"

[137] Gloster has already shown himself a believer in such astrological superstitions; so that Edmund here takes hold of him by just the right handle.

EDMUND. Look, sir, I bleed.
GLOUCESTER. Where is the villain, Edmund?
EDMUND. Fled this way, sir. When by no means he could—
GLOUCESTER. Pursue him, ho! Go after.—

[*Exeunt some* SERVANTS.]

       By no means what?
EDMUND. Persuade me to the murder of your lordship;
    But that I told him, the revenging gods
    'Gainst parricides did all their thunders bend;
    Spoke, with how manifold and strong a bond
    The child was bound to the father; sir, in fine,
    Seeing how loathly opposite I stood
    To his unnatural purpose, in fell motion,
    With his prepared sword, he charges home
    My unprovided body, lanced mine arm:
    But when he saw my best alarum'd spirits,
    Bold in the quarrel's right, roused to the encounter,
    Or whether gasted[138] by the noise I made,
    Full suddenly he fled.
GLOUCESTER. Let him fly far:
    Not in this land shall he remain uncaught;
    And, found, dispatch. The noble duke my master,
    My worthy arch[139] and patron, comes to-night:
    By his authority I will proclaim it,
    That he which finds him shall deserve our thanks,
    Bringing the murderous coward to the stake;
    He that conceals him, death.
EDMUND. When I dissuaded him from his intent,
    And found him pight to do it, with curst[140] speech
    I threaten'd to discover him: he replied,
    Thou unpossessing bastard! dost thou think,
    If I would stand against thee, would the reposal
    Of any trust, virtue, or worth in thee
    Make thy words faith'd? No: what I should deny,—
    As this I would: ay, though thou didst produce
    My very character,[141]*—I'd turn it all*

---

[138] That is, *aghasted, frighted.* So in Beaumont and Fletcher's *Wit at Several Weapons*: "Either the sight of the lady has *gasted* him, or else he's drunk."

[139] *Arch* is *chief*; still used in composition, as *arch-angel, arch-duke*, &c.

[140] *Plight* is *pitched, fixed*; *curst* is an epithet applied to any bad quality in excess; as a malignant, quarrelsome, or scolding temper. So in *The Taming of the Shrew*, Catharine is called "a *curst* shrew."

[141] *Character* here means *hand-writing* or *signature.*

To thy suggestion, plot, and damned practise:
And thou must make a dullard of the world,
If they not thought the profits of my death
Were very pregnant and potential spirits
To make thee seek it.
GLOUCESTER. Strong and fasten'd[142] villain
   Would he deny his letter? I never got him.

[Tucket within.]

   Hark, the duke's trumpets! I know not why he comes.
   All ports I'll bar; the villain shall not 'scape;
   The duke must grant me that: besides, his picture
   I will send far and near, that all the kingdom
   May have the due note of him; and of my land,
   Loyal and natural boy, I'll work the means
   To make thee capable.[143]

[Enter CORNWALL, REGAN, and ATTENDANTS.]

CORNWALL. How now, my noble friend! since I came hither,
   Which I can call but now, I have heard strange news.
REGAN. If it be true, all vengeance comes too short
   Which can pursue the offender. How dost, my lord?
GLOUCESTER. O, madam, my old heart is crack'd, it's crack'd!
REGAN. What, did my father's godson seek your life?
   He whom my father named? your Edgar?[144]
GLOUCESTER. O, lady, lady, shame would have it hid!
REGAN. Was he not companion with the riotous knights
   That tend upon my father?
GLOUCESTER. I know not, madam. 'Tis too bad, too bad.
EDMUND. Yes, madam, he was of that consort.
REGAN. No marvel, then, though he were ill affected:
   'Tis they have put him on the old man's death,
   To have the expense and waste of his revenues.
   I have this present evening from my sister

---

[142] *Strong* and *fasten'd* is *resolute and confirmed.* Strong was often used in a bad sense, as *strong* thief, *strong* traitor.

[143] That is, capable of succeeding to his estate. By law, Edmund was incapable of the inheritance. The word *natural* is here used with great art in the double sense of *illegitimate* and as opposed to *unnatural*, which latter epithet is implied upon Edgar.

[144] There is a peculiar subtlety and intensity of malice in these speeches of Regan. Coleridge justly observes that she makes "no reference to the guilt, but only to the accident, which she uses as an occasion for sneering at her father." And he adds, "Regan is not, in fact, a greater monster than Goneril, but she has the power of casting more venom."

Been well inform'd of them; and with such cautions,
That if they come to sojourn at my house,
I'll not be there.
CORNWALL. Nor I, assure thee, Regan.—
Edmund, I hear that you have shown your father
A child-like office.
EDMUND. 'Twas my duty, sir.
GLOUCESTER. He did bewray[145] his practise; and received
This hurt you see, striving to apprehend him.
CORNWALL. Is he pursued?
GLOUCESTER. Ay, my good lord.
CORNWALL. If he be taken, he shall never more
Be fear'd of doing harm: make your own purpose,
How in my strength you please.—For you, Edmund,
Whose virtue and obedience doth this instant
So much commend itself, you shall be ours:
Natures of such deep trust we shall much need;
You we first seize on.
EDMUND. I shall serve you, sir,
Truly, however else.
GLOUCESTER. For him I thank your grace.
CORNWALL. You know not why we came to visit you,—
REGAN. Thus out of season, threading[146] dark-eyed night:
Occasions, noble Gloucester, of some poise,[147]
Wherein we must have use of your advice:
Our father he hath writ, so hath our sister,
Of differences, which I least thought it fit
To answer from our home:[148] the several messengers
From hence attend dispatch. Our good old friend,
Lay comforts to your bosom; and bestow
Your needful counsel to our business,
Which craves the instant use.
GLOUCESTER. I serve you, madam:
Your graces are right welcome. [*Exeunt.*]

---

[145] *Bewray* is nearly the same in sense as *betray*, and means *disclose* or *reveal*. So in St. Matthew, xxvi. 73: "Thy speech *bewrayeth* thee."

[146] *Threading* is *passing through*. The word *dark-eyed* shows that an allusion to the threading of a needle was intended.

[147] *Poise* is *weight, importance*.—Regan's snatching the speech out of her husband's mouth is rightly in character. These two strong-minded ladies think nobody else can do any thing so well as they.

[148] That is, *away* from our home; from some other place than home.

SCENE II.

Before GLOUCESTER's *castle.*

[*Enter* KENT *and* OSWALD, *severally.*]

OSWALD. Good dawning[149] to thee, friend: art of this house?
KENT. Ay.
OSWALD. Where may we set our horses?
KENT. I' the mire.
OSWALD. Prithee, if thou lovest me, tell me.
KENT. I love thee not.
OSWALD. Why, then, I care not for thee.
KENT. If I had thee in Finsbury pinfold,[150] I would make thee care for
  me.
OSWALD. Why dost thou use me thus? I know thee not.
KENT. Fellow, I know thee.
OSWALD. What dost thou know me for?
KENT. A knave; a rascal; an eater of broken meats; a base, proud,
  shallow, beggarly, three-suited, hundred-pound, filthy, worsted-
  stocking knave; a lily-livered, action-taking knave, a whoreson,
  glass-gazing, super-serviceable finical rogue; one-trunk-inheriting
  slave; one that wouldst be a bawd, in way of good service, and art
  nothing but the composition of a knave, beggar, coward, pander,
  and the son and heir of a mongrel bitch: one whom I will beat into
  clamorous whining, if thou deniest the least syllable of thy
  addition.[151]
OSWALD. Why, what a monstrous fellow art thou, thus to rail on one
  that is neither known of thee nor knows thee!
KENT. What a brazen-faced varlet art thou, to deny thou knowest me!
  Is it two days ago since I tripped up thy heels, and beat thee before

---

[149] *Dawning* occurs again in *Cymbeline*, as substantive, for *morning*. It is still so
dark, however, that Oswald does not recognize Kent. Kent probably knows him by the
voice.
   [150] *Pinfold* is an old word for *pound*, a public enclosure where stray pigs and cattle
are shut up, to be bought out by the owner.
   [151] *Addition*, again, for *title*, but here put for the foregoing string of titles. A few of
these may need to be explained. "*Three-suited* knave" probably means one who spends
all he has, or his whole income, in dress. Kent afterwards says to Oswald, "a *tailor made*
thee." So in Jonson's *Silent Woman*: "Wert a pitiful fellow, and hadst nothing but three
suits of apparel." "Worsted-stocking knave" is another reproach of the same kind.
"Action-taking" is one who, if you beat him, would bring an action for assault, instead of
resenting it like a man of pluck. "One-trunk-inheriting,"—*inherit* in its old sense of to
own or *possess*. *Superservicenble* is about the same as *servile*; one that *overdoes* his
service; *sycophantic*. *Lily-liver'd* was a common epithet for a *coward*.—"A bawd," &c.,
may be one who does good service in the capacity of a bawd.

the King? Draw, you rogue: for, though it be night, yet the moon shines; I'll make a sop o' the moonshine of you.[152] [*Drawing his sword.*] Draw, you whoreson cullionly barber-monger,[153] draw!

OSWALD. Away! I have nothing to do with thee.

KENT. Draw, you rascal: you come with letters against the King; and take vanity the puppet's part[154] against the royalty of her father: draw, you rogue, or I'll so carbonado[155] your shanks: draw, you rascal; come your ways.

OSWALD. Help, ho! murder! help!

KENT. Strike, you slave; stand, rogue, stand; you neat slave,[156] strike! [*Beating him.*]

OSWALD. Help, ho! murder! murder!

[*Enter EDMUND, sword in hand.*]

EDMUND. How now! What's the matter? [*Parting them.*]

KENT. With you, goodman boy,[157] an you please: come, I'll flesh ye;[158] come on, young master.

[*Enter GLOSTER.*]

GLOUCESTER. Weapons! arms! What's the matter here?

[*Enter CORNWALL, REGAN, and SERVANTS.*]

CORNWALL. Keep peace, upon your lives:
He dies that strikes again. What is the matter?

---

[152] An equivoque is here intended, by an allusion to the old dish of *eggs in moonshine*, which was eggs broken and boiled in salad oil till the yolks became hard. It is equivalent to the phrase of modern times, "I'll *baste you*," or "*beat you to a mummy.*"

[153] Called *barber-monger* because he spends so much time in nursing his whiskers, in getting himself up, and in being barbered.

[154] Alluding, probably, to the old moral plays, in which the virtues and vices were personified. Vanity was represented as a female; and *puppet* was often a term of contempt for a woman. Jonson, in *The Devil is an Ass*, speaks of certain vices as "Lady Vanity" and "Old Iniquity."

[155] To *carbonado* is to *slash with stripes*, as a piece of meat to be cooked.

[156] Steevens thought that *neat slave* might mean, "you *finical* rascal, you assemblage of *foppery* and *poverty.*" Walker, a better authority, explains it, "*Neat* in the sense of *pure, unmixed;* still used in the phrase *neat wine.*" This makes it equivalent to "you *unmitigated villain.*"

[157] Kent purposely takes Edmund's *matter* in the sense of *quarrel*, and means, "I'll fight with you, if you wish it."—*Goodman*, in old usage, is about the same as *master* or *mister*. With *boy*, it is contemptuous. The word occurs repeatedly in the Bible; as "the *goodman* of the house."

[158] To *flesh* one is to give him his first trial in fighting, or to put him to the first proof of his valour. So in *King Henry IV., Part 1*, v. 4: "Full bravely hast thou *fleshed* thy maiden sword."

REGAN. The messengers from our sister and the King.

CORNWALL. What is your difference? speak.

OSWALD. I am scarce in breath, my lord.

KENT. No marvel, you have so bestirred your valour. You cowardly
rascal, nature disclaims in thee:[159] a tailor made thee.

CORNWALL. Thou art a strange fellow: a tailor make a man?

KENT. Ay, a tailor, sir: a stone-cutter[160] or painter could not have made
him so ill, though he had been but two hours at the trade.

CORNWALL. Speak yet, how grew your quarrel?

OSWALD. This ancient ruffian, sir, whose life I have spared at suit of
his gray beard,—

KENT. Thou whoreson zed![161] thou unnecessary letter! My lord, if you
will give me leave, I will tread this unbolted villain into mortar,[162]
and daub the wall of a jakes with him. Spare my gray beard, you
wagtail?[163]

CORNWALL. Peace, sirrah!
You beastly knave, know you no reverence?

KENT. Yes, sir; but anger hath a privilege.

CORNWALL. Why art thou angry?

KENT. That such a slave as this should wear a sword,
Who wears no honesty. Such smiling rogues as these,
Like rats, oft bite the holy cords a-twain
Which are too intrinse t' unloose;[164] smooth every passion
That in the natures of their lords rebel;[165]
Bring oil to fire, snow to their colder moods;
Renege, affirm, and turn their halcyon beaks
With every gale[166] and vary of their masters,

---

[159] That is, "Nature *disowns* thee." To *disclaim in* was often used for to *disclaim*
simply. Bacon has it so in his *Advancement of Learning.*—It would seem from this
passage, that Oswald is one whose "soul is in his clothes." Hence fond of being barbered
and curled and made fine.

[160] *Stone-cutter* for *sculptor,* or an artist in marble.

[161] *Zed* is here used as a term of contempt, because Z is the last letter in the English
alphabet: it is said to be an unnecessary letter, because its place may be supplied by S.
Ben Jonson, in his *English Grammar,* says "Z is a letter often heard among us, but
seldom seen."

[162] *Unbolted* is *unsifted,* hence *coarse.* The Poet has *bolted* repeatedly in the
opposite sense of *refined* or *pure.*

[163] *Wagtail,* I take it, comes pretty near meaning *puppy.*

[164] The image is of a knot so *intricate,* that it cannot be untied. The Poet uses
intrinsicate as another form of *intrinse,* in *Antony and Cleopatra,* v. 2: "With thy sharp
teeth this knot *intrinsicate* of life at once untie."

[165] To *smooth* is, here, to *cosset* or *flatter;* a common usage in the Poet's time.—
Rebel is here used as agreeing with the nearest substantive, instead of with the proper
subject, *That.*

[166] *Reneag* is *renounce* or *deny.* So in *Antony and Cleopatra,* i. 1: "His captain's
heart *reneags* all temper." It is commonly spelt *renege,* and sometimes *reneg.*—The
halcyon is a bird called the kingfisher, which, when dried and hung up by a thread, was

Knowing nought, like dogs, but following.—
A plague upon your epileptic visage![167]
Smile you my speeches, as I were a Fool?
Goose, if I had you upon Sarum plain,
I'd drive ye cackling home to Camelot.[168]

CORNWALL. Why, art thou mad, old fellow?

GLOUCESTER. How fell you out? say that.

KENT. No contraries hold more antipathy
Than I and such a knave.

CORNWALL. Why dost thou call him a knave? What's his offence?

KENT. His countenance likes me not.

CORNWALL. No more, perchance, does mine, nor his, nor hers.

KENT. Sir, 'tis my occupation to be plain:
I have seen better faces in my time
Than stands on any shoulder that I see
Before me at this instant.

CORNWALL. This is some fellow,
Who, having been praised for bluntness, doth affect
A saucy roughness, and constrains the garb
Quite from his nature:[169] he cannot flatter, he,
An honest mind and plain, he must speak truth!
An they will take it, so; if not, he's plain.
These kind of knaves I know, which in this plainness
Harbour more craft and more corrupter ends
Than twenty silly ducking observants
That stretch their duties nicely.[170]

KENT. Sir, in good sooth, in sincere verity,
Under the allowance of your great aspect,

---

supposed to turn its bill towards the point whence the wind blew. So in Marlowe's *Jew of Malta*: "But now how stands the wind? into what corner peers my halcyon's bill?"

[167] A visage distorted by grinning, as the next line shows.

[168] *Sarum* is an old contraction of *Salisbury*. Salisbury plain is the largest piece of flat surface in England, and used to be much noted as a lonely and desolate region.— *Camelot* is said to be a place in Somersetshire where large numbers of geese were bred. Old romances also make it the place where King Arthur kept his Court in the West. "Here, therefore," says Dyce, "there is perhaps a double allusion,—to Camelot as famous for its geese, and to those knights who were vanquished by the Knights of the Round Table being sent to Camelot to yield themselves as vassals to King Arthur."

[169] Forces his outside, or his appearance, to something totally *different* from his natural disposition.—*Garb* is used repeatedly by Shakespeare in the sense of *style* or *manner*.

[170] *Nicely* is *punctiliously*, with over-*strained nicety*.—Coleridge has a just remark upon this speech: "In thus placing these profound general truths in the mouths of such men as Cornwall, Edmund, Iago, &c., Shakespeare at once gives them utterance, and yet shows how indefinite their application is." I may add, that an inferior dramatist, instead of making his villains use any such vein of original and profound remark, would probably fill their mouths with something either shocking or absurd; which is just what real villains, if they have any wit, never do.

Whose influence, like the wreath of radiant fire
On flickering Phœbus' front,—
CORNWALL. What mean'st by this?
KENT. To go out of my dialect, which you discommend so much. I
    know, sir, I am no flatterer: he that beguiled you in a plain accent
    was a plain knave; which for my part I will not be, though I should
    win your displeasure to entreat me to't.
CORNWALL. What was the offence you gave him?
OSWALD. I never gave him any:
    It pleased the King his master very late
    To strike at me, upon his misconstruction;
    When he, conjunct and flattering his displeasure,
    Tripp'd me behind; being down, insulted, rail'd,
    And put upon him such a deal of man,
    That worthied him, got praises of the King
    For him attempting who was self-subdued;[171]
    And, in the fleshment of this dread exploit,
    Drew on me here again.
KENT. None of these rogues and cowards
    But Ajax is their Fool.[172]
CORNWALL. Fetch forth the stocks!—
    You stubborn ancient knave, you reverend braggart,
    We'll teach you—
KENT. Sir, I am too old to learn:
    Call not your stocks for me: I serve the King;
    On whose employment I was sent to you:
    You shall do small respect, show too bold malice
    Against the grace and person of my master,
    Stocking his messenger.
CORNWALL. Fetch forth the stocks!—As I have life and honour,
    There shall he sit till noon.
REGAN. Till noon! till night, my lord; and all night too.
KENT. Why, madam, if I were your father's dog,
    You should not use me so.
REGAN. Sir, being his knave, I will.
CORNWALL. This is a fellow of the self-same colour
    Our sister speaks of.—Come, bring away the stocks!

[*Stocks brought out.*]

---

[171] By "him who was self-subdued," Oswald means himself, pretending that the
poor figure he made was the result of virtuous self-control, and not of imbecility or
fear.—*Fleshment* here means *pride* or *elation*; or, as we say, *flushed*.

[172] Ajax is a fool to them. "These rogues and cowards talk in such a boasting strain
that, if we were to credit their account of themselves, Ajax would appear a person of no
prowess when *compared* to them."

GLOUCESTER. Let me beseech your grace not to do so:
    His fault is much, and the good King his master
    Will cheque him for't: your purposed low correction
    Is such as basest and contemned'st wretches
    For pilferings and most common trespasses
    Are punish'd with: the King must take it ill,
    That he's so slightly valued in his messenger,
    Should have him thus restrain'd.
CORNWALL. I'll answer that.
REGAN. My sister may receive it much more worse,
    To have her gentleman abused, assaulted,
    For following her affairs.—Put in his legs.—

[KENT *is put in the stocks.*]

Come, my good lord, away.

[*Exeunt all but* GLOUCESTER *and* KENT.]

GLOUCESTER. I am sorry for thee, friend; 'tis the duke's pleasure,
    Whose disposition, all the world well knows,
    Will not be rubb'd[173] nor stopp'd: I'll entreat for thee.
KENT. Pray, do not, sir: I have watched and travell'd hard;
    Some time I shall sleep out, the rest I'll whistle.
    A good man's fortune may grow out at heels:[174]
    Give you good morrow!
GLOUCESTER. The duke's to blame in this; 'twill be ill taken. [*Exit.*]
KENT. Good King, that must approve[175] the common saw,
    Thou out of Heaven's benediction comest
    To the warm sun![176]—
    Approach, thou beacon to this under globe,
    That by thy comfortable beams I may

---

[173] *Rubb'd* is *impeded* or *hindered.* A rub in a bowling-alley is something that obstructs or deflects the bowl.

[174] A man set in the stocks was said to be "punished by the heels"; and Kent probably alludes to this. He also means, apparently, that the fortune even of a good man may have holes in the heels of its shoes; or, as we say, may be "out at the toes," or "out at the elbows."

[175] Here, again, to *approve* is to *make good,* to *prove true,* to *confirm.*

[176] The *saw,* that is, the *saying* or *proverb,* alluded to is, "Out of God's blessing into the warm sun"; which was used to signify the state of one cast out from the comforts and charities of home, and left exposed to the social inclemencies of the world. Lyly, in his *Euphues,* has an apt instance of the proverb reversed: "Therefore, if thou wilt follow my advice, and prosecute thine owne determination, thou shalt come out of a warm Sunne into God's blessing."

Peruse this letter!—Nothing almost sees miracles
But misery.[177] I know 'tis from Cordelia,
Who hath most fortunately been inform'd
Of my obscured course; and shall find time
From this enormous state, seeking to give
Losses their remedies.[178] All weary and o'erwatch'd,
Take vantage, heavy eyes, not to behold
This shameful lodging.—
Fortune, good night: smile once more: turn thy wheel! [*Sleeps.*]

SCENE III.

The open Country.

[*Enter* EDGAR.]

EDGAR. I heard myself proclaim'd;
And by the happy[179] hollow of a tree
Escaped the hunt. No port is free; no place,
That guard, and most unusual vigilance,
Does not attend my taking. Whiles I may 'scape,
I will preserve myself: and am bethought
To take the basest and most poorest shape
That ever penury, in contempt of man,
Brought near to beast: my face I'll grime with filth;
Blanket my loins: elf all my hair in knots;[180]

---

[177] That is, hardly any but the miserable see miracles. Here *see* probably means *experience*,—a sense in which it is often used. Kent appears to be thinking of the supernatural cures and acts of beneficence recorded in the Gospels, where indeed miracles are almost never wrought but in behalf of the wretched; and upon this thought he seems to be building a hope of better times, both for himself and the old King; while, on the other hand, nothing short of a miraculous providence seems able to turn their course of misfortune.

[178] I here adopt the arrangement and explanation proposed to me by Mr. Joseph Crosby. The verbs *know* and *shall find* are in the same construction: "I know, and I shall find." *Enormous* is used in its proper Latin sense of *abnormal, anamalous*, or *out of rule*; and refers to Kent's own situation, his "obscured course." So, in the Shakespeare portion of *The Two Noble Kinsmen*, v. 1, Mars is addressed, "O great corrector of *enormous* times, shaker of o'er-rank States." So that the meaning comes thus: "From this anomalous state of mine, I shall gain time to communicate and co-operate with Cordelia in her endeavour to restore the kingdom to its former condition; 'to give losses their remedies,' that is, to reinstate Lear on the throne, Cordelia in his favour, and myself in his confidence, and in my own rights and titles." All this Kent utters in a disjointed way, because half-asleep; and then, having viewed the situation as hopefully as he can, he puts up a prayer to Fortune, and drops off to sleep.

[179] Here, as often, *happy* is *propitious* or *lucky*; like the Latin *felix*.

[180] The entangling and knotting of the hair was supposed to be done by elves and fairies in the night; hence called *elf-knots*.

And with presented nakedness out-face
The winds and persecutions of the sky.
The country gives me proof and precedent
Of Bedlam beggars,[181] who, with roaring voices,
Strike in their numb'd and mortified bare arms
Pins, wooden pricks, nails, sprigs of rosemary;
And with this horrible object, from low farms,
Poor pelting[182] villages, sheep-cotes, and mills,
Sometime with lunatic bans,[183] sometime with prayers,
Enforce their charity. *Poor Turlygod!*[184] *Poor Tom!*
That's something yet: Edgar I nothing am. [*Exit.*]

SCENE IV.

Before GLOUCESTER'*s Castle*; KENT *in the stocks.*

[*Enter* KING LEAR, FOOL, *and a* GENTLEMAN.]

KING LEAR. 'Tis strange that they should so depart from home,
And not send back my messenger.
GENTLEMAN. As I learn'd,
The night before there was no purpose in them
Of this remove.
KENT. Hail to thee, noble master!
KING LEAR. Ha!
Makest thou this shame thy pastime?
KENT. No, my lord.
FOOL. Ha, ha! he wears cruel[185] garters. Horses are tied by the heads,
dogs and bears by the neck, monkeys by the loins, and men by the

---

[181] In *The Bell-Man of London*, by Dekker, 1640, is an account of one of these characters, under the title of *Abraham Man*: "He sweares he hath been in Bedlam, and will talke frantickely of purpose: you see *pinnes* stuck in sundry places of his naked flesh, especially in his *armes*, which paine he gladly puts himselfe to, only to make you believe he is out of his wits. He calls himselfe by the name of *Poore Tom*, and, coming near any body, cries out, *Poor Tom is a-cold.*"

[182] *Pelting* is *paltry* or *insignificant.*

[183] *Bans* is *curses.* The Poet had no doubt often seen such lunatics roving about in obscure places, and extorting pittances here and there, sometimes by loud execrations, sometimes by petitionary whinings.

[184] *Turlygood* appears to have been a corruption of *Turlupin*, a name applied to a fanatical sect that overran France, Italy, and Germany in the 13th and 14th centuries. "Their manners and appearance," says Douce, "exhibited the strongest indications of lunacy and distraction. The common people called them Turlupins. Their subsequent appellation of the fraternity of poor men might have been the cause why the wandering rogues called Bedlam beggars, one of whom Edgar personates, assumed or obtained the title of *Turlupins* or *Turlygoods.*"

[185] A quibble between *cruel* and *crewel*; the latter being worsted.

legs: when a man's over-lusty at legs, then he wears wooden
nether-stocks.[186]

KING LEAR. What's he that hath so much thy place mistook
To set thee here?

KENT. It is both he and she;
Your son and daughter.

KING LEAR. No.

KENT. Yes.

KING LEAR. No, I say.

KENT. I say, yea.

KING LEAR. No, no, they would not.

KENT. Yes, they have.

KING LEAR. By Jupiter, I swear, no.

KENT. By Juno, I swear, ay.

KING LEAR. They durst not do't;
They could not, would not do't; 'tis worse than murder,
To do upon respect[187] such violent outrage:
Resolve me,[188] with all modest haste, which way
Thou mightst deserve, or they impose, this usage,
Coming from us.

KENT. My lord, when at their home
I did commend your highness' letters to them,
Ere I was risen from the place that show'd
My duty kneeling, came there a reeking post,
Stew'd in his haste, half breathless, panting forth
From Goneril his mistress salutations;
Deliver'd letters, spite of intermission,[189]
Which presently they read: on whose contents,
They summon'd up their meiny,[190] straight took horse;
Commanded me to follow, and attend
The leisure of their answer; gave me cold looks:
And meeting here the other messenger,
Whose welcome, I perceived, had poison'd mine,—
Being the very fellow that of late
Display'd so saucily against your highness,—
Having more man than wit about me, drew:[191]

---

[186] *Nether-stocks* is the old word for what we call *stockings.*

[187] The meaning probably is, to do *deliberately,* or upon *consideration.* See page 27, note 42.

[188] "*Resolve* me" is *inform* me or *assure* me. A frequent usage.

[189] That is, *in* spite of the *interruption* or *delay* naturally consequent upon what Kent was himself doing. In other words, the "reeking post" did not heed Kent's action at all, nor allow himself to be delayed by it. *Intermission* occurs both in *The Merchant* and in *Macbeth* for *pause* or *delay,* which is nearly its meaning here.

[190] "On *reading* the contents *of which*" is the meaning.—*Meiny* is from a French word meaning *household,* or *retinue.*

He raised the house with loud and coward cries.
Your son and daughter found this trespass worth
The shame which here it suffers.
FOOL. Winter's not gone yet, if the wild-geese fly that way.[192]

> Fathers that wear rags
> > Do make their children blind;
> But fathers that bear bags
> > Shall see their children kind.
> Fortune, that arrant whore,
> Ne'er turns the key to th' poor.—

But, for all this, thou shalt have as many dolours[193] for thy
daughters as thou canst tell in a year.
KING LEAR. O, how this mother[194] swells up toward my heart!
Hysterica passio, down, thou climbing sorrow,
Thy element's below!—Where is this daughter?
KENT. With the earl, sir, here within.
KING LEAR. Follow me not;
Stay here. [*Exit.*]
GENTLEMAN. Made you no more offence but what you speak of?
KENT. None.
How chance the King comes with so small a train?
FOOL. And thou hadst been set i' the stocks for that question, thou
hadst well deserved it.
KENT. Why, Fool?
FOOL. We'll set thee to school to an ant, to teach thee there's no
labouring i' the Winter.[195] All that follow their noses are led by
their eyes but blind men; and there's not a nose among twenty but
can smell him that's stinking.[196] Let go thy hold when a great

---

[191] The pronoun *I* is understood here from the fourth line above.

[192] "If such is their behaviour, the King's troubles are not over yet."

[193] A quibble between dolours and dollars.—Tell, in the next line, is count, and refers to dollars.

[194] Lear affects to pass off the swelling of his heart, ready to burst with grief and indignation, for the disease called the *mother*, or *hysterica passio*, which, in the Poet's time, was not thought peculiar to women.

[195] Referring to Proverbs, vi. 6-8: "Go to the ant, thou sluggard; consider her ways, and be wise; which having no guide overseer, or ruler, provideth her meat in the Summer, and gathereth her food in the harvest." And the application is, "If you had learned of the ant, you would have known that the King's train are too shrewd to be making hay in cloudy weather, or to think of providing their meat when the Winter of adversity has set in.

[196] All but blind men are led by their eyes, though they follow their noses; and these, seeing the King's forlorn condition, have forsaken him; while even of the blind, who have nothing but their noses to guide them, there is not one in twenty but can smell him who, being "muddy in Fortune's mood, smells somewhat strong of her displeasure."

wheel runs down a hill, lest it break thy neck with following it: but
the great one that goes up the hill, let him draw thee after. When a
wise man gives thee better counsel, give me mine again: I would
have none but knaves follow it, since a Fool gives it.

>   That sir which serves and seeks for gain,
>   And follows but for form,
>   Will pack when it begins to rain,
>   And leave thee in the storm,
>   But I will tarry; the Fool will stay,
>   And let the wise man fly:
>   The knave turns Fool that runs away;
>   The Fool no knave, perdy.[197]

KENT. Where learned you this, Fool?
FOOL. Not i' the stocks, Fool.

[*Re-enter* KING LEAR, *with* GLOUCESTER.]

KING LEAR. Deny to speak with me? They are sick? they are weary?
    They have travell'd all the night? Mere fetches;[198]
    The images of revolt and flying off.
    Fetch me a better answer.
GLOUCESTER. My dear lord,
    You know the fiery quality of the duke;
    How unremoveable and fix'd he is
    In his own course.
KING LEAR. Vengeance! plague! death! confusion!
    Fiery? what quality? Why, Gloucester, Gloucester,
    I'd speak with the Duke of Cornwall and his wife.
GLOUCESTER. Well, my good lord, I have inform'd them so.
KING LEAR. Inform'd them! Dost thou understand me, man?
GLOUCESTER. Ay, my good lord.
KING LEAR. The King would speak with Cornwall; the dear father
    Would with his daughter speak, commands her service:[199]

It is to be noted that the Fool does not know Kent, and therefore cannot conceive the
motive of his action; so here, in characteristic fashion, he is satirizing Kent's adherence to
the King, as showing him to be without either sight or smell; that is, as having no sense at
all.

[197] Here the Fool may be using the trick of suggesting a thing by saying its opposite.
Or perhaps he is playing upon the two senses of knave, one of which is *servant*. This
would infer who the real fools in the world are. Coleridge says "a knave is a fool with a
circumbendibus."

[198] *Fetch* was often used for *device, pretext*, or *stratagem*.

[199] Lear is here asserting something of the regal authority which he has abdicated;
and his meaning depends somewhat on an emphasizing of the words *King, commands,*

Are they inform'd of this? My breath and blood!
Fiery? the fiery duke? Tell the hot duke that—
No, but not yet: may be he is not well:
Infirmity doth still neglect all office
Whereto our health is bound; we are not ourselves
When nature, being oppress'd, commands the mind
To suffer with the body: I'll forbear;
And am fall'n out with my more headier will,
To take[200] the indisposed and sickly fit
For the sound man.—[*Looking on* KENT.]
    Death on my state! wherefore
Should he sit here? This act persuades me
That this remotion[201] of the duke and her
Is practise only. Give me my servant forth.
Go tell the duke and's wife I'd speak with them,
Now, presently: bid them come forth and hear me,
Or at their chamber-door I'll beat the drum
Till it cry sleep to death.[202]

GLOUCESTER. I would have all well betwixt you. [*Exit.*]
KING LEAR. O me, my heart, my rising heart! but, down!
FOOL. Cry to it, nuncle, as the cockney[203] did to the eels when she put
    'em i' the paste alive; she knapped 'em o' the coxcombs with a
    stick, and cried *Down, wantons, down!* 'Twas her brother that, in
    pure kindness to his horse, buttered his hay.

[*Enter* CORNWALL, REGAN, GLOUCESTER, *and Servants.*]

KING LEAR. Good morrow to you both.
CORNWALL. Hail to your grace!

[KENT *is set at liberty.*]

REGAN. I am glad to see your highness.
KING LEAR. Regan, I think you are; I know what reason

---

and *service*.
    [200] The infinitive *to take* is here used *gerundively*, or like the Latin *gerund*, and so is
equivalent to *in taking*.—Here the Poet follows a well-known Latin idiom, using the
comparative *more headier*, in the sense of *too* heady, that is, too *headlong*.
    [201] *Remotion* for *removal*; referring to Cornwall and Regan's action in *departing*
from home.
    [202] That is, till it kills sleep with noise and clamour.
    [203] The etymology, says Nares, seems most probable, which derives *cockney* from
cookery. Le pays de cocagne, or *coquaine*, in old French, means a country of good cheer.
This *Lubberland*, as Florio calls it, seems to have been proverbial for the simplicity or
gullibility of its inhabitants. Dekker, in his *Newes from Hell*, says, "'Tis not our fault; but
our mothers, our *cockering* mothers, who for their labour made us to be called *cockneys*."

I have to think so: if thou shouldst not be glad,
I would divorce me from thy mother's tomb,
Sepulchring an adultress.—[*to* KENT.] O, are you free?
Some other time for that.—Beloved Regan,
Thy sister's naught: O Regan, she hath tied
Sharp-tooth'd unkindness, like a vulture, here:

[*Points to his heart.*]

I can scarce speak to thee; thou'lt not believe
With how depraved a quality—O Regan!
REGAN. I pray you, sir, take patience: I have hope.
      You less know how to value her desert
      Than she to scant her duty.[204]
KING LEAR. Say, how is that?
REGAN. I cannot think my sister in the least
      Would fail her obligation: if, sir, perchance
      She have restrain'd the riots of your followers,
      'Tis on such ground, and to such wholesome end,
      As clears her from all blame.
KING LEAR. My curses on her!
REGAN. O, sir, you are old.
      Nature in you stands on the very verge
      Of her confine: you should be ruled and led
      By some discretion, that discerns your state
      Better than you yourself. Therefore, I pray you,
      That to our sister you do make return;
      Say you have wrong'd her, sir.
KING LEAR. Ask her forgiveness?
      Do you but mark how this becomes the House:[205]
      [*Kneeling.*] *Dear daughter, I confess that I am old;*
      Age is unnecessary:[206] *on my knees I beg*
      That you'll vouchsafe me raiment, bed, and food.

---

[204] There is something of perplexity here. Taken strictly, the passage can only mean, "She knows *better* how to *be wanting* in her duty than you know how to value her desert"; which is clearly the reverse of the sense intended. The difficulty grows from putting a positive and a negative clause together in a comparison. Change the positive clause into a negative, and the sense comes right, thus: "You know *not* how to value her desert, *rather than* she knows how to be wanting in her duty." Still better, perhaps, if we change the negative clause into a positive: "You less know how to value her desert than she knows how to *do* her duty."

[205] How it comports with the order of the family or of the domestic relations, that the father should be a kneeling suppliant to the child.

[206] *Unnecessary*, here, is commonly explained as meaning *necessitous*, or *without the necessaries of life*. But the more probable explanation takes Lear as giving an ironical apology for the uselessness of his existence. "An old man, such as I am, can be of no use to any one, and so must be content to live upon alms."

REGAN. Good sir, no more; these are unsightly tricks:
    Return you to my sister.
KING LEAR. [*Rising.*] Never, Regan:
    She hath abated me of half my train;
    Look'd black upon me; struck me with her tongue,
    Most serpent-like, upon the very heart:
    All the stored vengeances of Heaven fall
    On her ingrateful top! Strike her young bones,
    You taking airs, with lameness!
CORNWALL. Fie, sir, fie!
KING LEAR. You nimble lightnings, dart your blinding flames
    Into her scornful eyes! Infect her beauty,
    You fen-suck'd fogs, drawn by the powerful sun,
    To fall[207] and blast her pride!
REGAN. O the blest gods! so will you wish on me,
    When the rash mood is on.
KING LEAR. No, Regan, thou shalt never have my curse:
    Thy tender-hefted[208] nature shall not give
    Thee o'er to harshness: her eyes are fierce; but thine
    Do comfort and not burn. 'Tis not in thee
    To grudge my pleasures, to cut off my train,
    To bandy hasty words, to scant my sizes,[209]
    And in conclusion to oppose the bolt
    Against my coming in: thou better know'st
    The offices of nature, bond of childhood,
    Effects of courtesy, dues of gratitude;
    Thy half o' the kingdom hast thou not forgot,
    Wherein I thee endow'd.
REGAN. Good sir, to the purpose.
KING LEAR. Who put my man i' the stocks? [*Tucket within.*]
CORNWALL. What trumpet's that?
REGAN. I know't,—my sister's: this approves her letter,
    That she would soon be here.—

[*Enter* OSWALD.]

---

[207] *Fall* is here a transitive verb, meaning *take down* or *abase.*

[208] The best explanation of this is given in *The Edinburgh Review*, July, 1869: "*Heft* is a well-known older English word for *handle*, that which holds or contains; and *tender-hefted* is simply *delicately housed, finely sheathed. Heft* was in this way applied proverbially to the body; and Howell has a phrase, quoted by Halliwell, which is a good example of its graphic use,—'loose in the heft,'—to designate an ill habit of body, a person of dissipated ways. *Tender-hefted* is, therefore, *tender-bodied, delicately-organized*, or, more literally, *finely-fleshed.*"

[209] A *size* is a *portion* or *allotment* of food. The term *sizer* is still used at the English universities for students living on a stated allowance.

Is your lady come?

KING LEAR. This is a slave, whose easy-borrow'd pride
    Dwells in the fickle grace of her he follows.[210]—
    Out, varlet, from my sight!

CORNWALL. What means your grace?

KING LEAR. Who stock'd my servant? Regan, I have good hope
    Thou didst not know on't. Who comes here?—O Heavens,

[*Enter* GONERIL.]

If you do love old men, if your sweet sway
Allow[211] obedience, if yourselves are old,
Make it your cause; send down, and take my part!
[*To* GONERIL.] Art not ashamed to look upon this beard?
O Regan, wilt thou take her by the hand?

GONERIL. Why not by the hand, sir? How have I offended?
    All's not offence that indiscretion finds
    And dotage terms so.

KING LEAR. O sides, you are too tough;
    Will you yet hold?—How came my man i' the stocks?

CORNWALL. I set him there, sir: but his own disorders
    Deserved much less advancement.

KING LEAR. You! did you?

REGAN. I pray you, father, being weak, seem so.[212]
    If, till the expiration of your month,
    You will return and sojourn with my sister,
    Dismissing half your train, come then to me:
    I am now from home, and out of that provision
    Which shall be needful for your entertainment.

KING LEAR. Return to her, and fifty men dismiss'd?
    No, rather I abjure all roofs, and choose
    To wage against the enmity o' the air;
    To be a comrade with the wolf and owl,—
    Necessity's sharp pinch![213] Return with her?

---

[210] Whose pride depends upon, or *comes and goes* with the shifting *favour* of his mistress; who puts on airs or falls his crest according as she smiles or frowns upon him.

[211] To *allow* in its old sense of *approve.* So in the 11th Psalm of *The Psalter:* "The Lord *alloweth* the righteous."

[212] "Since you are weak, be content to think yourself so."

[213] "Necessity's sharp pinch" is of course the pain of hunger or of cold. So, later in this play, we have "the *belly-pinched* wolf," to signify the same pain. Shakespeare seems rather fond of the word *howl,* to express the shrieks or outcries of human want or pain or anguish. So in *Macbeth,* iv. 3: "Each morn new widows *howl;* new orphans cry." And again: "I have words that would be *howl'd* out in the desert air." Also in *Henry the Fifth,* iii. 2: "Whiles the mad mothers with their *howls* confused do break the clouds." And in *Hamlet,* v. 1 "A ministering angel shall my sister be, when thou liest *howling.*" I do not

Why, the hot-blooded France, that dowerless took
Our youngest born, I could as well be brought
To knee his throne, and, squire-like; pension beg
To keep base life afoot. Return with her?
Persuade me rather to be slave and sumpter[214]
To this detested groom. [*Pointing at* OSWALD.]
GONERIL. At your choice, sir.
KING LEAR. I prithee, daughter, do not make me mad:
I will not trouble thee, my child; farewell:
We'll no more meet, no more see one another:
But yet thou art my flesh, my blood, my daughter;
Or rather a disease that's in my flesh,
Which I must needs call mine: thou art a boil,
A plague-sore, an embossed[215] carbuncle,
In my corrupted blood. But I'll not chide thee;
Let shame come when it will, I do not call it:
I do not bid the thunder-bearer shoot,
Nor tell tales of thee to high-judging Jove.[216]
Mend when thou canst; be better at thy leisure:
I can be patient; I can stay with Regan,
I and my hundred knights.
REGAN. Not altogether so:
I look'd not for you yet, nor am provided
For your fit welcome. Give ear, sir, to my sister;
For those that mingle reason with your passion
Must be content to think you old, and so—
But she knows what she does.
KING LEAR. Is this well spoken?
REGAN. I dare avouch it, sir: what, fifty followers?
Is it not well? What should you need of more?
Yea, or so many, sith[217] that both charge and danger
Speak 'gainst so great a number? How, in one house,
Should many people, under two commands,
Hold amity? 'Tis hard; almost impossible.
GONERIL. Why might not you, my lord, receive attendance

---

understand Lear to mean that he would literally cohabit or herd with wolves, but merely that he would be like them, or in the same condition with them, in this respect, that he would roam at large, homeless, roofless, and submit to such extremities of hunger and cold as would force him to bowl forth his need of food and warmth.

[214] *Sumpter* is used along with *horse* or *mule*, to signify one that carries provisions or other necessaries.

[215] *Embossed* is *swollen* or *protuberant*; like the boss of a shield.

[216] "The Thunder-bearer" is the same as Jove the Thunderer. So that *Nor* connects "do not bid" and "tell tales."

[217] *Sith* and *sithence* were old forms just falling out of use in the Poet's time, and now entirely superseded by *since*.

From those that she calls servants or from mine?
REGAN. Why not, my lord? If then they chanced to slack you,
    We could control them. If you will come to me,—
    For now I spy a danger,—I entreat you
    To bring but five and twenty: to no more
    Will I give place or notice.
KING LEAR. I gave you all—
REGAN. And in good time you gave it.[218]
KING LEAR. Made you my guardians, my depositaries;
    But kept a reservation to be follow'd
    With such a number. What, must I come to you
    With five and twenty, Regan? said you so?
REGAN. And speak't again, my lord; no more with me.
KING LEAR. Those wicked creatures yet do look well-favour'd,
    When others are more wicked: not being the worst
    Stands in some rank of praise.—[*to* GONERIL.] I'll go with thee:
    Thy fifty yet doth double five and twenty,
    And thou art twice her love.
GONERIL. Hear me, my lord;
    What need you five and twenty, ten, or five,
    To follow in a house where twice so many
    Have a command to tend you?
REGAN. What need one?
KING LEAR. O, reason not the need: our basest beggars
    Are in the poorest thing superfluous:
    Allow not nature more than nature needs,
    Man's life's as cheap as beast's: thou art a lady;
    If only to go warm were gorgeous,
    Why, nature needs not what thou gorgeous wear'st,
    Which scarcely keeps thee warm.[219] But, for true need,—
    You Heavens, give me that patience, patience I need!
    You see me here, you gods, a poor old man,
    As full of grief as age; wretched in both!

---

[218] This spurt of malice, snapped in upon Lear's pathetic appeal, is the *ne plus ultra* of human fiendishness. This cold, sharp venom of retort is what chiefly distinguishes Regan from Goneril: otherwise they seem too much like repetitions of each other to come fairly within the circle of Nature, who never repeats herself. Professor Dowden discriminates these intellectual and strong-minded girls as follows: "The two terrible creatures are distinguishable. Goneril is the calm wielder of a pitiless force, the resolute initiator of cruelty. Regan is a smaller, shriller, fiercer, more eager piece of malice. The tyranny of the elder sister, is a cold, persistent pressure, as little affected by tenderness or scruple as the action of some crushing hammer; Regan's ferocity is more unmeasured, and less abnormal or monstrous."

[219] The scope of this reasoning seems to be, "You need clothing only for warmth; yet you pile up expense of dress for other ends, while your dress, after all, hardly meets that natural want; which shows that you would rather suffer lack of warmth than of personal adornment."

If it be you that stir these daughters' hearts
Against their father, Fool me not so much
To bear it tamely; touch me with noble anger,
And let not women's weapons, water-drops,
Stain my man's cheeks!—No, you unnatural hags,
I will have such revenges on you both,
That all the world shall—I will do such things,—
What they are, yet I know not: but they shall be
The terrors of the earth. You think I'll weep
No, I'll not weep:
I have full cause of weeping; but this heart
Shall break into a hundred thousand flaws,[220]
Or ere I'll weep.—O Fool, I shall go mad!

[*Exeunt* KING LEAR, GLOUCESTER, KENT, *and* FOOL. *Storm heard at a distance.*]

CORNWALL. Let us withdraw; 'twill be a storm.
REGAN. This house is little: the old man and his people
　　Cannot be well bestow'd.
GONERIL. 'Tis his own blame; hath put himself from rest,
　　And must needs taste his folly.
REGAN. For his particular, I'll receive him gladly,
　　But not one follower.
GONERIL. So am I purposed.
　　Where is my lord of Gloucester?
CORNWALL. Follow'd the old man forth: he is return'd.

[*Re-enter* GLOUCESTER.]

GLOUCESTER. The King is in high rage.
CORNWALL. Whither is he going?
GLOUCESTER. He calls to horse; but will I know not whither.
CORNWALL. 'Tis best to give him way; he leads himself.
GONERIL. My lord, entreat him by no means to stay.[221]
GLOUCESTER. Alack, the night comes on, and the bleak winds
　　Do sorely ruffle; for many miles a bout
　　There's scarce a bush.
REGAN. O, sir, to wilful men,
　　The injuries that they themselves procure
　　Must be their schoolmasters. Shut up your doors:

---

[220] *Flaws* formerly signified *fragments*, as well as mere *cracks*. The word, as Bailey observes, was "especially applied to the breaking off *shivers* or thin pieces from precious stones."

[221] "Do not by any means entreat him to stay," is the meaning.

He is attended with a desperate train;
And what they may incense him to, being apt
To have his ear abused, wisdom bids fear.
CORNWALL. Shut up your doors, my lord; 'tis a wild night:
My Regan counsels well; come out o' the storm. [*Exeunt.*]

ACT III.

SCENE I.

A Heath. A Storm, with Thunder and Lightning.

[*Enter* KENT *and a* GENTLEMAN, *meeting.*]

KENT. Who's there, besides foul weather?
GENTLEMAN. One minded like the weather, most unquietly.
KENT. I know you. Where's the King?
GENTLEMAN. Contending with the fretful elements:
    Bids the winds blow the earth into the sea,
    Or swell the curled water 'bove the main,[222]
    That things might change or cease; tears his white hair,
    Which the impetuous blasts, with eyeless rage,
    Catch in their fury, and make nothing of;
    Strives in his little world of man to out-scorn
    The to-and-fro-conflicting wind and rain.
    This night, wherein the cub-drawn bear would couch,
    The lion and the belly-pinched wolf[223]
    Keep their fur dry, unbonneted he runs,
    And bids what will take all.
KENT. But who is with him?
GENTLEMAN. None but the Fool; who labours to out-jest
    His heart-struck injuries.
KENT. Sir, I do know you;
    And dare, upon the warrant of my note,[224]
    Commend a dear thing to you. There is division,
    Although as yet the face of it be cover'd
    With mutual cunning, 'twixt Albany and Cornwall;
    Who have—as who have not, that their great stars

---

[222] Lear wishes for the destruction of the world, either by the winds blowing the land into the water, or raising the waters so as to overwhelm the land.

[223] A bear made fierce by suckling her cubs; a wolf enraged by the gnawings of hunger.

[224] *Note* for *notice, knowledge,* or *observation;* referring to "I do *know* you." Shakespeare repeatedly uses *note* thus. Here, as in divers other places, *commend* has the sense of *commit.*

Throned and set high?—servants, who seem no less,
Which are to France the spies and speculations
Intelligent of our State;[225] what hath been seen,
Either in snuffs and packings of the dukes,[226]
Or the hard rein which both of them have borne
Against the old kind King; or something deeper,
Whereof perchance these are but furnishings.[227]
But, true it is, from France there comes a power
Into this scatter'd kingdom;[228] who already,
Wise in our negligence, have secret feet[229]
In some of our best ports, and are at point
To show their open banner. Now to you:
If on my credit you dare build so far
To make your speed to Dover, you shall find
Some that will thank you, making just report
Of how unnatural and bemadding sorrow
The King hath cause to plain.
I am a gentleman of blood and breeding;
And, from some knowledge and assurance, offer
This office to you.
GENTLEMAN. I will talk further with you.
KENT. No, do not.
For confirmation that I am much more
Than my out-wall, open this purse, and take
What it contains. If you shall see Cordelia,—
As fear not but you shall,—show her this ring;
And she will tell you who your fellow is[230]
That yet you do not know. Fie on this storm!
I will go seek the King.
GENTLEMAN. Give me your hand: have you no more to say?
KENT. Few words, but, to effect, more than all yet;
That, when we have found the King,—in which your pain
That way, I'll this,[231]—he that first lights on him

---

[225] "Who seem the servants of Albany and Cornwall, but are really engaged in the service of France as spies, gathering and conveying information of all that is done here." *Intelligent* here carries the sense not only of *knowing*, but also of *giving intelligence*; *intelligencers.—Speculator* in the Latin sense of *observer* or *looker-on.*

[226] *Snuffs* are dislikes, and *packings* underhand contrivances.

[227] That is, whereof these things are but the trimmings or appendages; not the thing itself, but only the circumstances or *furniture* of the thing.

[228] That is, having its *military force* scattered; or, perhaps, *distracted* by the feud between Albany and Cornwall.

[229] Have secret *footing*; have *landed secretly.—At point*, next line, is *ready* or *prepared*; *on the point of showing*, as we should say.

[230] *Fellow* was often used for *companion.*

[231] "In which search you take pains in that direction, and I will in this."

Holla the other. [*Exeunt severally.*]

SCENE II.

Another part of the heath. Storm still.

[*Enter* KING LEAR *and* FOOL.]

KING LEAR. Blow, winds, and crack your cheeks! rage! blow!
 You cataracts and hurricanoes,[232] spout
 Till you have drench'd our steeples, drown'd the cocks!
 You sulphurous and thought-executing fires,[233]
 Vaunt-couriers to oak-cleaving thunderbolts,
 Singe my white head! And thou, all-shaking thunder,
 Smite flat the thick rotundity o' the world!
 Crack nature's moulds, an germens spill at once,[234]
 That make ingrateful man!

FOOL. O nuncle, court holy-water[235] in a dry house is better than this
 rain-water out o' door. Good nuncle, in, and ask thy daughters'
 blessing: here's a night pities neither wise man nor Fool.

KING LEAR. Rumble thy bellyful! Spit, fire! spout, rain!
 Nor rain, wind, thunder, fire, are my daughters:
 I tax not you, you elements, with unkindness;
 I never gave you kingdom, call'd you children,
 You owe me no subscription:[236] then let fall
 Your horrible pleasure: here I stand, your slave,
 A poor, infirm, weak, and despised old man:
 But yet I call you servile ministers,
 That have with two pernicious daughters join'd
 Your high engender'd battles 'gainst a head
 So old and white as this. O! O! 'tis foul!

FOOL. He that has a house to put's head in has a good head-piece.

---

[232] *Hurricano* was the seaman's term for what we call a *water-spout*. So in *Troilus and Cressida*, v. 2: "Not the dreadful spout, which shipmen do the *hurricano* call, constringed in mass by the almighty Sun, shall dizzy with more clamour Neptune's ear in his descent," &c.—A *cataract* is any flood of falling water, whether from the sky or over a precipice.

[233] *Thought-executing* may mean acting with the swiftness of thought, or executing the thoughts of Jupiter *Tonans.—Vaunt-couriers* originally meant the foremost scouts of an army, as lightning foreruns thunder.

[234] There is a parallel passage in *The Winter's Tale*, iv. 3: "Let Nature crush the sides o' the Earth together, and mar the *seeds* within."

[235] Court *holy-water* is fair words and flattering speeches. So Chillingworth, in one of his sermons: "Can any man think so unworthily of our Saviour, as to esteem these words of His for no better than *compliment*? for nothing but *court holy-water*?"

[236] Are under no oath or obligation of service of kindness to me. Referring to the binding force of one's signature. See page 31, note 55.

The cod-piece[237] that will house
   Before the head has any,
The head and he shall louse;
   So beggars marry many.[238]
The man that makes his toe
   What he his heart should make
Shall of a corn cry *Woe!*[239]
   And turn his sleep to wake.

For there was never yet fair woman but she made mouths in a glass.[240]

KING LEAR. No, I will be the pattern of all patience;
I will say nothing.

[*Enter* KENT.]

KENT. Who's there?

FOOL. Marry, here's grace and a cod-piece;[241] that's a wise man and a Fool.

KENT. Alas, sir, are you here? things that love night
Love not such nights as these; the wrathful skies
Gallow[242] the very wanderers of the dark,
And make them keep their caves: since I was man,
Such sheets of fire, such bursts of horrid thunder,
Such groans of roaring wind and rain, I never

---

[237] *Codpiece* was the coarse name given to an indelicate part of masculine attire, now out of use. It was very conspicuous, and was used for sticking pins and carrying the purse in, &c.

[238] I am not clear whether this means that many beggars marry, or that a beggar has many bedfellows. Pehaps the saying of Sir Hugh Evans will fit the case: "The dozen white louses do become an old coat well: it is a familiar beast to man, and signifies love."

[239] A covert allusion to the King. Making the heart and the toe change places with each other is the Fool's characteristic figure for such an inversion of things as Lear has made in setting his daughters above himself. Perhaps Mr. Furness's comment is right: "The meaning, if it be worth a search, seems to be this: 'A man who prefers or cherishes a mean member in place of a vital one shall suffer enduring pain where others would suffer merely a twinge.' Lear had preferred Regan and Goneril to Cordelia."

[240] This is the Fool's way of diverting attention after he has said something a little too pointed: the idea of a very pretty woman making faces in a looking-glass raises a smile.—FURNESS.

[241] Meaning the King and himself; *Grace* being a common title of royalty.— "Shakespeare," says Douce, "has with some humour applied codpiece to the Fool, who was usually provided with this unseemly part of dress in a more remarkable manner than other persons."

[242] To *gallow* is to *frighten*, to *terrify*. The word is exceedingly rare; though the form *gally* is said to be used in the West of England. And Huntley, in his *Glossary of the Cotswold Dialect*, has "Gallow. To alarm; to frighten."

    Remember to have heard: man's nature cannot carry
    The affliction nor the fear.[243]
KING LEAR. Let the great gods,
    That keep this dreadful pother o'er our heads,
    Find out their enemies now. Tremble, thou wretch,
    That hast within thee undivulged crimes,
    Unwhipp'd of justice: hide thee, thou bloody hand;
    Thou perjured, and thou simular[244] man of virtue
    That art incestuous: caitiff, to pieces shake,
    That under covert and convenient seeming
    Hast practised on man's life: close pent-up guilts,
    Rive your concealing continents,[245] and cry
    These dreadful summoners grace.[246] I am a man
    More sinn'd against than sinning.
KENT. Alack, bare-headed!
    Gracious my lord, hard by here is a hovel;
    Some friendship will it lend you 'gainst the tempest:
    Repose you there; while I to this hard house—
    More harder than the stones whereof 'tis raised;
    Which even but now, demanding after you,
    Denied me to come in—return, and force
    Their scanted courtesy.
KING LEAR. My wits begin to turn.—
    Come on, my boy: how dost, my boy? art cold?
    I am cold myself. Where is this straw, my fellow?
    The art of our necessities is strange,
    That can make vile things precious.[247] Come, your hovel.—
    Poor Fool and knave, I have one part in my heart
    That's sorry yet for thee.

---

[243] *Affliction* for *infliction;* then equivalent terms. Man's nature cannot endure the infliction, nor even the fear of it. So in the Prayer-Book: "Defend us from all dangers and mischiefs, and from the fear of them."

[244] *Simular* for *simulator.* A simulator is one who puts on the show of what he is not, as a *dissimulator* puts off the show of what he is.

[245] *Continent* for that which *contains* or *encloses.* So in *Antony and Cleopatra,* iv. 14: "Heart, once be stronger than thy *continent.*"

[246] *Summoners* are officers that summon offenders for trial or punishment. To *cry grace* is to beg for mercy or pardon. Lear is regarding the raging elements as the agents or representatives of the gods, calling criminals to judgment.

[247] An allusion to alchemy, which was supposed to have the power of transmuting vile metals into precious, as lead into gold.

FOOL.

[*Sings.*]

He that has and[248] *a little tiny wit—*
   With hey, ho, the wind and the rain,—
Must make content with his fortunes fit,
   For the rain it raineth every day.

KING LEAR. True, my good boy. Come, bring us to this hovel.

[*Exeunt* KING LEAR *and* KENT.]

FOOL. This is a brave night to cool a courtezan. I'll speak a prophecy
   ere I go:

     When priests are more in word than matter;
     When brewers mar their malt with water;
     When nobles are their tailors' tutors;
     No heretics burn'd, but wenches' suitors;
     When every case in law is right;
     No squire in debt, nor no poor knight;
     When slanders do not live in tongues;
     Nor cutpurses[249] come not to throngs;
     When usurers tell[250] their gold i' the field;
     And bawds and whores do churches build;
     Then shall the realm of Albion
     Come to great confusion:
     Then comes the time, who lives to see't,
     That going shall be used with feet.

This prophecy Merlin shall make;[251] for I live before his time.
[*Exit.*]

---

[248] In old ballads, *and* is sometimes, as here, apparently redundant, but adds a slight force to the expression, like *even.*

[249] *Cutpurses* were the same as what we call *pickpockets.*

[250] To *tell, again,* in the old sense of to *count.* See page 63, note 193.

[251] Merlin was a famous prophet in the Druidical mythology of ancient Britain, who did divers wonderful things "by his deep science and Hell-dreaded might." Some of his marvels are sung in *The Faerie Queene,* iii. 2, 18-21. Part of his prophecy, which the Fool here anticipates, is given in Puttenham's *Art of Poetry,* 1589.

SCENE III.

A Room in GLOUCESTER'*s Castle.*

[*Enter* GLOUCESTER *and* EDMUND.]

GLOUCESTER. Alack, alack, Edmund, I like not this unnatural dealing. When I desire their leave that I might pity him, they took from me the use of mine own house; charged me, on pain of their perpetual displeasure, neither to speak of him, entreat for him, nor any way sustain him.

EDMUND. Most savage and unnatural!

GLOUCESTER. Go to; say you nothing. There is a division betwixt the dukes; and a worse matter than that: I have received a letter this night; 'tis dangerous to be spoken; I have locked the letter in my closet: these injuries the King now bears will be revenged home;[252] there's part of a power already footed: we must incline to the King. I will seek him, and privily relieve him: go you and maintain talk with the duke, that my charity be not of him perceived: if he ask for me. I am ill, and gone to bed. Though I die for it, as no less is threatened me, the King my old master must be relieved. There is some strange thing toward, Edmund; pray you, be careful. [*Exit.*]

EDMUND. This courtesy, forbid thee![253] shall the duke
    Instantly know; and of that letter too:
    This seems a fair deserving, and must draw me
    That which my father loses; no less than all:
    The younger rises when the old doth fall. [*Exit.*]

---

[252] Here, as often, *home* has the sense of *thoroughly, to the utmost.* So, again, in the next scene: "But I will punish *home.*"

[253] "*Forbid* thee" I take to mean "*A curse upon* thee," or like our phrase, "*Confound* you." So in *Macbeth*, i. 3, we have "He shall live a man *forbid*"; that is, shall live *under a curse* or *an interdict*; pursued by an evil fate. Mr. Crosby, however, takes *forbid* in the sense merely of *forbidden*, and as agreeing with *courtesy.* In this case, the reference of course would be to the aid and comfort which Gloster resolves to give the old King, notwithstanding the threats of Cornwall and Regan. It may be so: but does not this make the sense too tame?

SCENE IV.

The Heath, near a Hovel. Storm continues.

[*Enter* KING LEAR, KENT, *and the* FOOL.[254]]

KENT. Here is the place, my lord; good my lord, enter:
    The tyranny of the open night's too rough
    For nature to endure.
KING LEAR. Let me alone.
KENT. Good my lord, enter here.
KING LEAR. Wilt break my heart?
KENT. I had rather break mine own. Good my lord, enter.
KING LEAR. Thou think'st 'tis much that this contentious storm
    Invades us to the skin: so 'tis to thee;
    But where the greater malady is fix'd,
    The lesser is scarce felt. Thou'dst shun a bear;
    But if thy flight lay toward the raging sea,
    Thou'dst meet the bear i' the mouth. When the mind's free,
    The body's delicate: the tempest in my mind
    Doth from my senses take all feeling else
    Save what beats there. Filial ingratitude!
    Is it not as this mouth should tear this hand
    For lifting food to't? But I will punish home:
    No, I will weep no more. In such a night
    To shut me out!—Pour on; I will endure;—
    In such a night as this! O Regan, Goneril!
    Your old kind father, whose frank heart gave all,—
    O, that way madness lies; let me shun that;
    No more of that.
KENT. Good my lord, enter here.
KING LEAR. Prithee, go in thyself: seek thine own ease:
    This tempest will not give me leave to ponder
    On things would hurt me more. But I'll go in.—
    In, boy; go first.—You houseless poverty,—
    Nay, get thee in. I'll pray, and then I'll sleep.—

---

[254] O, what a world's convention of agonies is here! All external Nature in a storm, all moral nature convulsed,—the real madness of Lear, the feigned madness of Edgar, the babbling of the Fool, the desperate fidelity of Kent,—surely such a scene was never conceived before or since! Take it but as a picture for the eye only, it is more terrific than any which a Michael Angelo, inspired by a Dante, could have conceived, and which none but a Michael Angelo could have executed. Or let it have been uttered to the blind, the howlings of nature would seem converted into the voice of conscious humanity.— COLERIDGE.

[*The* FOOL *goes in.*]

Poor naked wretches, whereso'er you are,
That bide the pelting of this pitiless storm,
How shall your houseless heads and unfed sides,
Your loop'd and window'd[255] raggedness, defend you
From seasons such as these? O, I have ta'en
Too little care of this! Take physic, pomp;
Expose thyself to feel what wretches feel,
That thou mayst shake the superflux to them,
And show the Heavens more just.
EDGAR. [*Within.*] Fathom and half, fathom and half! Poor Tom!

[*The* FOOL *runs out from the hovel.*]

FOOL. Come not in here, nuncle, here's a spirit
    Help me, help me!
KENT. Give me thy hand.—Who's there?
FOOL. A spirit, a spirit: he says his name's poor Tom.
KENT. What art thou that dost grumble there i' the straw?
    Come forth.

[*Enter* EDGAR *disguised as a madman.*]

EDGAR. Away! the foul fiend follows me![256]

Through the sharp hawthorn blows the cold wind.

Hum! go to thy cold bed, and warm thee.[257]
KING LEAR. Hast thou given all to thy two daughters?
    And art thou come to this?
EDGAR. Who gives any thing to poor Tom? whom the foul fiend hath
    led through fire and through flame, and through ford and

---

[255] *Loop'd* and *window'd* is full of *holes* and *apertures.* The allusion is to loop-holes, such as are found in ancient castles, and designed for the admission of light and air.

[256] Edgar's assumed madness serves the great purpose of taking off part of the shock which would otherwise be caused by the true madness of Lear, and further displays the profound difference between the two. In Edgar's ravings Shakespeare all the while lets you see a fixed purpose, a practical end in view; in Lear's, there is only the brooding of the one anguish, an eddy without progression.—COLERIDGE.

[257] This appears to have been a sort of proverbial phrase. Shakespeare has it again in *The Taming of the Shrew.* Staunton quotes, from *The Spanish Tragedy,* "What outcries pluck me from my *naked* bed?" and says, "The phrase *to go to a cold bed* meant only to *go cold to bed*; to *rise from a naked bed* signified to *get up naked from bed.*"

whirlipool e'er bog and quagmire;[258] that hath laid knives under his pillow, and halters in his pew; set ratsbane by his porridge;[259] made film proud of heart, to ride on a bay trotting-horse over four-inched bridges, to course his own shadow for a traitor. Bless thy five wits![260] Tom's a-cold. O, do de, do de, do de.[261] Bless thee from whirlwinds, star-blasting, and taking![262] Do poor Tom some charity, whom the foul fiend vexes: there could I have him now,—and there,—and there again, and there. [*Storm continues.*]

KING LEAR. What, have his daughters brought him to this pass?—
Couldst thou save nothing? Didst thou give them all?

FOOL. Nay, he reserved a blanket, else we had been all shamed.

KING LEAR. Now, all the plagues that in the pendulous air
Hang fated o'er men's faults light on thy daughters!

KENT. He hath no daughters, sir.

KING LEAR. Death, traitor! nothing could have subdued nature
To such a lowness but his unkind daughters.
Is it the fashion, that discarded fathers
Should have thus little mercy on their flesh?
Judicious punishment! 'twas this flesh begot
Those pelican daughters.[263]

EDGAR. *Pillicock sat on Pillicock-hill*:[264]
Halloo, halloo, loo, loo!

FOOL. This cold night will turn us all to fools and madmen.

EDGAR. Take heed o' the foul fiend: obey thy parents; keep thy word justly; swear not; commit not with man's sworn spouse; set not thy sweet heart on proud array. Tom's a-cold.

KING LEAR. What hast thou been?

---

[258] Alluding to the *ignis fatuus*, supposed to be lights kindled by mischievous beings to lead travellers into destruction.

[259] Fiends were commonly represented as thus tempting the wretched to suicide. So in *Doctor Faustus*, 1604: "Swords, poisons, halters, and envenomed steel are laid before me, to dispatch myself."

[260] The five senses were sometimes called the *five wits*. And the mental powers, being supposed to correspond in number to the senses, were called the *five wits* also. The reference here is, probably, to the latter.

[261] These syllables are probably meant to represent the chattering of one who shivers with cold.

[262] To *take* is to strike with malignant influence. So in ii. 4 of this play: "Strike her young bones, you *taking* airs, with lameness!"

[263] The young pelican is fabled to suck the mother's blood. The allusions to this fable are very numerous in old writers.

[264] In illustration of this, Mr. Halliwell has pointed out the following couplet in *Gammer Gurton's Garland*:

Pillycock, Pillycock sat on a hill;
If he's not gone, he sits there still.

EDGAR. A serving-man, proud in heart and mind; that curled my hair; wore gloves in my cap;[265] served the lust of my mistress' heart, and did the act of darkness with her; swore as many oaths as I spake words, and broke them in the sweet face of Heaven: one that slept in the contriving of lust, and waked to do it: wine loved I deeply, dice dearly: and in woman out-paramoured the Turk: false of heart, light of ear,[266] bloody of hand; hog in sloth, fox in stealth, wolf in greediness, dog in madness, lion in prey. Let not the creaking of shoes nor the rustling of silks betray thy poor heart to woman: keep thy foot out of brothels, thy hand out of plackets,[267] thy pen from lenders' books, and defy the foul fiend.

> *Still through the hawthorn blows the cold wind*:
> *Says suum, mun, ha, no, nonny.*
> *Dolphin my boy, my boy, sessa! let him trot by.*[268]

[*Storm still.*]

KING LEAR. Why, thou wert better in thy grave than to answer with thy uncovered body this extremity of the skies. Is man no more than this? Consider him well. Thou owest the worm no silk, the beast no hide, the sheep no wool, the cat no perfume. Ha! here's three on's are sophisticated![269] Thou art the thing itself: unaccommodated man is no more but such a poor bare, forked animal as thou art.—Off, off, you lendings! come unbutton here.

[*Tearing off his clothes.*]

FOOL. Prithee, nuncle, be contented; 'tis a naughty night to swim in. Now a little fire in a wild field were like an old lecher's heart; a

---

[265] *Gloves* were anciently worn in the cap, either as the favour of a mistress, or as the memorial of a friend, or as a badge to be challenged.

[266] *Light of ear* means "sinning with the ear"; that is, greedy or credulous of slanders and malicious reports, or of obscene talk.

[267] Upon this troublesome word Mr. Grant White comments as follows: "It is clear that the placket, in Shakespeare's time and after, was an article of female apparel so secret as not to admit description, and so common as not to require it; and that, consequently, the thing having passed out of use, the word *stat nominis umbra.*"

[268] Much effort has been made to explain this strain of jargon; but it probably was not meant to be understood, its sense lying in its having no sense. And Edgar's counterfeit seems to proceed in part by stringing together odds and ends of old ballads, without connection or intelligible purpose. *Sessa* is elsewhere used by the Poet for *cease* or *be quiet. Dolphin* is the old form of *Dauphin*; and "Dolphin my boy, my boy, cease, let him trot by" is the burden of a ridiculous old song.

[269] Meaning himself, Kent, and the Fool; and they three are sophisticated out of nature in wearing clothes. Therefore, to become unsophisticated, he will off with his "lendings," and be as Edgar is.

small spark, all the rest on's body cold. Look, here comes a
walking fire.

EDGAR. This is the foul fiend Flibbertigibbet:[270] he begins at curfew,
and walks till the first cock; he gives the web and the pin,[271]
squints the eye, and makes the hare-lip; mildews the white wheat,
and hurts the poor creature of Earth.

> *Swithold footed thrice the old;*
> *He met the night-mare, and her nine-fold;*
> *Bid her alight, and her troth plight,[272]*
> *And, aroint thee, witch, aroint thee![273]*

KENT. How fares your Grace?

[*Enter* GLOSTER *with a torch.*]

KING LEAR. What's he?
KENT. Who's there? What is't you seek?
GLOUCESTER. What are you there? Your names?
EDGAR. Poor Tom; that eats the swimming frog, the toad, the tadpole,
the wall-newt and the water;[274] that in the fury of his heart, when
the foul fiend rages, eats cow-dung for sallets; swallows the old rat
and the ditch-dog; drinks the green mantle of the standing pool;
who is whipped from tithing to tithing, and stock-punished, and
imprison'd;[275] who hath had three suits to his back, six shirts to his

---

[270] The names of this fiend and most of the fiends mentioned by Edgar were found
in Harsnet's book. It was an old tradition that spirits were relieved from confinement at
the time of curfew, that is, at the close of the day, and were permitted to wander at large
till the first cock-crowing. Hence, in *The Tempest*, they are said to "rejoice to hear the
solemn curfew."

[271] "The web and the pin" is thus explained in Florio's *Dictionary*: "*Cataratta*,—a
dimnesse of sight occasioned by humores hardned in the eies, called a Cataract, or a pin
and a web." Also in Cotgrave's *Dictionary*: "*Taye*,—any filme, or thinne skinne, &c.; and
hence a pin or web in the eye, a white filme overgrowing the eye."

[272] Who Saint Withold was is uncertain.—*Wold* is a plain open country, whether
hilly or not; formerly spelt *old, ould,* and *wold,* indifferently. *Nine-fold* is put for *nine
foals,* to rhyme with *wold.* The *troth-plight* here referred to was meant as a charm against
the *night-mare.*

[273] There is some diversity of opinion as to the origin and meaning of *aroint.* In
Macbeth, i. 3, "*Aroint* thee, witch," seems to be used as a charm against witchcraft; and
the angry threatenings of the Witch at having it pronounced to her look as if she had been
baffled by it. So that the more likely meaning seems to be, *stand off* or *be gone.*

[274] The wall-newt and the water-newt; small lizards.

[275] "From *tything* to *tything*" is from *parish* to *parish.* The severities inflicted on the
wretched beings, one of whom Edgar is here personating, are set forth in Harrison's
Description of England: "The rogue being apprehended, committed to prison, and tried at
the next assizes, if he be convicted for a vagabond, he is then adjudged to be grievously
whipped, and burned through the gristle of the right ear with a hot iron, as a manifestation
of his wicked life, and due punishment received for the same."

body, horse to ride, and weapon to wear;

> *But mice and rats, and such small deer,*
> *Have been Tom's food for seven long year.*[276]

Beware my follower.—Peace, Smulkin; peace, thou fiend!

GLOUCESTER. What, hath your grace no better company?

EDGAR. *The prince of darkness is a gentleman*:
    Modo he's call'd, and Mahu.[277]

GLOUCESTER. Our flesh and blood is grown so vile, my lord,
    That it doth hate what gets it.[278]

EDGAR. Poor Tom's a-cold.

GLOUCESTER. Go in with me: my duty cannot suffer
    To obey in all your daughters' hard commands:
    Though their injunction be to bar my doors,
    And let this tyrannous night take hold upon you,
    Yet have I ventured to come seek you out,
    And bring you where both fire and food is ready.

KING LEAR. First let me talk with this philosopher.
    What is the cause of thunder?

KENT. Good my lord, take his offer; go into the house.

KING LEAR. I'll talk a word with this same learned Theban.—
    What is your study?

EDGAR. How to prevent the fiend, and to kill vermin.

KING LEAR. Let me ask you one word in private.

KENT. Importune him once more to go, my lord;
    His wits begin to unsettle.

GLOUCESTER. Canst thou blame him?
    His daughters seek his death: ah, that good Kent!
    He said it would be thus, poor banish'd man!
    Thou say'st the King grows mad; I'll tell thee, friend,
    I am almost mad myself: I had a son,

---

[276] This couplet is founded on one in the old metrical romance of *Sir Bevis*, who was confined seven years in a dungeon:

> Rattes and myce and such smal dere
> Was his meate that seven yere.

[277] So in Harsnet's *Declaration*: "*Maho* was the chief devil that had possession of Sarah Williams; but another of the possessed, named Richard Mainy, was molested by a still more considerable fiend, called *Modu*." Again the said Richard Mainy deposes: "Furthermore it is pretended, that there remaineth still in mee the prince of devils, whose name should be *Modu*."—The two lines conclude a catch in *The Goblins*, a piece ascribed to Sir John Suckling.

[278] Gloster here alludes to his son Edgar, as well as to Lear's daughters; and this makes Edgar the more anxious for his disguise, lest his feelings should mar his counterfeiting. Hence he exclaims, "Poor Tom's a-cold."

Now outlaw'd from my blood; he sought my life,
But lately, very late: I loved him, friend;
No father his son dearer: truth to tell thee, [*Storm continues.*]
The grief hath crazed my wits. What a night's this!—
I do beseech your Grace,—

KING LEAR. O, cry your mercy,[279] sir.
Noble philosopher, your company.

EDGAR. Tom's a-cold.

GLOUCESTER. In, fellow, there, into the hovel: keep thee warm.

KING LEAR. Come let's in all.

KENT. This way, my lord.

KING LEAR. With him;
I will keep still with my philosopher.

KENT. Good my lord, soothe him; let him take the fellow.

GLOUCESTER. Take him you on.

KENT. Sirrah, come on; go along with us.

KING LEAR. Come, good Athenian.

GLOUCESTER. No words, no words: hush.

EDGAR.
>   *Child Rowland to the dark tower came,*
>   *His word was still, Fie, foh, and fum,*
>   *I smell the blood of a British man.*[280] [*Exeunt.*]

SCENE V.

A Room in GLOUCESTER'*s Castle.*

[*Enter* CORNWALL *and* EDMUND.]

CORNWALL. I will have my revenge ere I depart his house.

EDMUND. How, my lord, I may be censured, that nature thus gives
way to loyalty, something fears me to think of.

CORNWALL. I now perceive, it was not altogether your brother's evil
disposition made him seek his death; but a provoking merit, set a-
work by a reprovable badness in himself.[281]

---

[279] "I cry you mercy" is an old phrase for "I ask your pardon."

[280] Child Roland, that is, Knight Orlando, was reputed to be the youngest son of
King Arthur. Edgar, it seems, purposely disjoints his quotations, or leaves their sense
incomplete. In the ballad of *Jack and the Giants*, which, if not older than the play, may
have been compiled from something that was so, a giant lets off this:

>   Fee, faw, fum,
>   I smell the blood of an Englishman:
>   Be he alive, or be be dead,
>   I'll grind his bones to make my bread.

EDMUND. How malicious is my fortune, that I must repent to be just![282] This is the letter he spoke of, which approves him an intelligent party to the advantages of France: O Heavens! that this treason were not, or not I the detector!

CORNWALL. Go with me to the duchess.

EDMUND. If the matter of this paper be certain, you have mighty business in hand.[283]

CORNWALL. True or false, it hath made thee earl of Gloucester. Seek out where thy father is, that he may be ready for our apprehension.

EDMUND. [*Aside.*] If I find him comforting the King, it will stuff his suspicion more fully.—[*To* CORNWALL.] I will persevere in my course of loyalty, though the conflict be sore between that and my blood.

CORNWALL. I will lay trust upon thee; and thou shalt find a dearer father in my love. [*Exeunt.*]

SCENE VI.

A Chamber in a Farmhouse adjoining GLOUCESTER's *castle.*

[*Enter* GLOUCESTER, KING LEAR, KENT, FOOL, *and* EDGAR.]

GLOUCESTER. Here is better than the open air; take it thankfully. I will piece out the comfort with what addition I can: I will not be long from you.

KENT. All the power of his wits have given way to his impatience: the gods reward your kindness!

[*Exit* GLOUCESTER.]

---

[281] By a "provoking merit" Cornwall means, apparently, a virtue *apt to be provoked*, or *stirred into act*; which virtue was set to work by some flagrant evil in Gloster himself; and it was this, and not altogether a bad disposition in Edgar, that made Edgar seek the old man's life. Provoking for *provocable*; the active form with the passive sense. The Poet has a great many instances of such usage. Mr. Crosby, however, gives me a different interpretation; taking *merit* in the neutral sense of *desert*, as the word is sometimes so used. "It was not altogether your brother Edgar's evil disposition that made him seek his father's death: it was the old man's *desert* that *provoked* him to it; that is, the old man *deserved* it." Cornwall then attempts to soften his remark by saying that this "provoking merit" was set at work by a reprovable badness in Edgar himself; using the mild term *reprovable* in connection with the unfilial badness of a son in seeking his father's death, even though the father deserved it.

[282] "*To be* just" is another instance of the infinitive used gerundively, and is equivalent to *of being* just. See page 65, note 200.

[283] The "mighty business in hand" is a war; as the "paper" in question is a letter informing Gloster that an army had landed from France.

EDGAR. Frateretto calls me; and tells me Nero is an angler in the lake of darkness.—Pray, innocent,[284] and beware the foul fiend.

FOOL. Prithee, nuncle, tell me whether a madman be a gentleman or a yeoman?

KING LEAR. A King, a King!

FOOL. No, he's a yeoman that has a gentleman to his son; for he's a mad yeoman that sees his son a gentleman before him.[285]

KING LEAR. To have a thousand with red burning spits
Come hissing in upon 'em,—

EDGAR. The foul fiend bites my back.

FOOL. He's mad that trusts in the tameness of a wolf, a horse's health, a boy's love, or a whore's oath.

KING LEAR. It shall be done; I will arraign them straight.—
[*To* EDGAR.] Come, sit thou here, most learned justicer;[286]—
[*To the* FOOL.] Thou, sapient sir, sit here.—Now, you she foxes!—

EDGAR. Look, where he stands and glares!—Wantest thou eyes at trial, madam?[287]

Come o'er the bourn, Bessy, to me,—

FOOL.

Her boat hath a leak,
And she must not speak
Why she dares not come over to thee.[288]

---

[284] Rabelais says that Nero was a fiddler in Hell, and Trajan an angler. The history of Gargantua appeared in English before 1575. *Fools* were anciently termed *innocents*.

[285] A rather curious commentary on some of the Poet's own doings; who obtained from the Heralds' College a coat-of-arms in his father's name; thus getting his yeoman father dubbed a gentleman, in order, no doubt, that himself might inherit the rank.

[286] *Justicer* is the older and better word for what we now call a justice.

[287] When Edgar says, "Look, where he stands and glares!" he seems to be speaking in the character of a madman, who thinks he sees the fiend. "Wantest thou eyes at trial, madam?" is addressed to some visionary person who is supposed, apparently, to be on trial, but does not see the spectre.

[288] *Bourn* here means a brook or rivulet, as streams of all sorts were apt to be taken for *boundaries*. These four lines are probably from an old song, which was imitated by Birch in his *Dialogue between Elizabeth and England*; the imitation beginning thus:

Come over the bourn, Bessy, come over the bourn, Bessy,
Sweet Bessy, come over to me;
And I shall thee take, and my dear lady make
Before all that ever I see.

EDGAR. The foul fiend haunts poor Tom in the voice of a nightingale.
Hoppedance cries in Tom's belly for two white herring.—Croak
not, black angel; I have no food for thee.

KENT. How do you, sir? Stand you not so amazed:
Will you lie down and rest upon the cushions?

KING LEAR. I'll see their trial first.—Bring in the evidence.—
[*To* EDGAR.] Thou robed man of justice, take thy place;—
[*To the* FOOL.] And thou, his yoke-fellow of equity,
Bench by his side.—[*To* KENT.] you are o' the commission,
Sit you too.

EDGAR. Let us deal justly.

> *Sleepest or wakest thou, jolly shepherd?*
>> *Thy sheep be in the corn;*
>> *And for one blast of thy minikin*[289] *mouth,*
>> *Thy sheep shall take no harm.*

Purr! the cat is gray.[290]

KING LEAR. Arraign her first; 'tis Goneril. I here take my oath before
this honourable assembly, she kicked the poor King her father.

FOOL. Come hither, mistress. Is your name Goneril?

KING LEAR. She cannot deny it.

FOOL. Cry you mercy, I took you for a joint-stool.[291]

KING LEAR. And here's another, whose warp'd looks proclaim
What store her heart is made on.—Stop her there!
Arms, arms, sword, fire! Corruption in the place!
False justicer, why hast thou let her 'scape?[292]

EDGAR. Bless thy five wits!

KENT. O pity!—Sir, where is the patience now,
That thou so oft have boasted to retain?

EDGAR. [*Aside.*] My tears begin to take his part so much,
They'll mar my counterfeiting.

---

[289] *Minikin* was a term of fondness or endearment. Baret's *Alvearie* has "neate, fresh, pretie, fine, *minikin*, tricke and trimme."

[290] The meaning of *Pur* is any thing but obvious. But *Purre* is the name of a devil in Harsnet. So perhaps the name suggests the purring of a cat, and of a cat *too old to sing.*

[291] This appears to have been a proverbial expression. It occurs again, somewhat modified, in *King Henry IV., Part 1*, ii. 4: "Thy state is taken for a joint-stool." It is also met with in various other old writings. It was the name of what we call a *folding-chair*; a chair with a *joint* in it.

[292] It does not seem probable that Shakespeare wished to represent Lear as the subject of so extreme an hallucination as that his daughters were present, in their own figure and appearance, and that one of them escaped. It is more probable that he wished to represent them, personified by the excited imagination, in the form of stools; and that Kent or Edgar, seeing the bad effects which this vivid personification was working, snatched away one of the stools; and this produces the passionate explosion on Regan's supposed escape.—DR. BUCKNILL.

KING LEAR. The little dogs and all,
    Tray, Blanch, and Sweet-heart, see, they bark at me.
EDGAR. Tom will throw his head at them. Avaunt, you curs!

> Be thy mouth or black or white,
> Tooth that poisons if it bite;
> Mastiff, grey-hound, mongrel grim,
> Hound or spaniel, brach or lym,[293]
> Or bobtail tike or trundle-tail,
> Tom will make them weep and wail:
> For, with throwing thus my head,
> Dogs leap the hatch, and all are fled.

Do de, de, de. Sessa! Come, march to wakes and fairs and market-
towns.—Poor Tom, thy horn is dry.[294]
KING LEAR. Then let them anatomize Regan; see what breeds about
    her heart. Is there any cause in nature that makes these hard
    hearts?—[*To* EDGAR.] You, sir, I entertain for one of my
    hundred; only I do not like the fashion of your garments: you will
    say they are Persian attire: but let them be changed.[295]
KENT. Now, good my lord, lie here and rest awhile.
KING LEAR. Make no noise, make no noise; draw the curtains: so, so,
    so. We'll go to supper i' he morning. So, so, so.
FOOL. And I'll go to bed at noon.[296]

[*Re-enter* GLOUCESTER.]

GLOUCESTER. Come hither, friend: where is the King my master?
KENT. Here, sir; but trouble him not, his wits are gone.
GLOUCESTER. Good friend, I prithee, take him in thy arms;
    I have o'erheard a plot of death upon him:
    There is a litter ready; lay him in't,
    And drive towards Dover, friend, where thou shalt meet

---

[293] A *lym* or *lyme* was a *hound*; sometimes also called a *limmer* or *leamer* , from the *leam* or *leash*, in which he was held till he was let slip.

[294] A *horn* was usually carried by every Tom of Bedlam, to receive such drink as the charitable might afford him, with whatever scraps of food they might give him. So Edgar begs to have his horn filled.

[295] Lear is comparatively tranquil in conduct and language during the whole period of Edgar's mad companionship. It is only after the Fool has disappeared,—gone to sleep at midday, as he says,—and Edgar has left, to be the guide of his blind father, that the King becomes absolutely wild and incoherent. Few things tranquillize the insane more than the companionship of the insane. It is a fact not easily explicable; but it is one of which, either by the intuition of genius or by the information of experience, Shakespeare appears to have been aware.—DR. BUCKNILL.

[296] These words are the last we have from the Fool. They are probably meant as a characteristic notice that the poor fellow's heart is breaking.

Both welcome and protection. Take up thy master:
If thou shouldst dally half an hour, his life,
With thine, and all that offer to defend him,
Stand in assured loss: take up, take up;
And follow me, that will to some provision
Give thee quick conduct.

KENT. Oppressed nature sleeps:
This rest might yet have balm'd thy broken senses,
Which, if convenience[297] will not allow,
Stand in hard cure.[298]—[*To the* FOOL.] Come, help to bear thy
    master;
Thou must not stay behind.

GLOUCESTER. Come, come, away.

[*Exeunt* KENT, GLOSTER, *and the* FOOL, *bearing off* LEAR.]

EDGAR. When we our betters see bearing our woes,
We scarcely think our miseries our foes.
Who alone suffers suffers most i' the mind,
Leaving free things and happy shows behind;
But then the mind much sufferance doth o'er skip,
When grief hath mates, and bearing fellowship.
How light and portable my pain seems now,
When that which makes me bend makes the King bow,
He childed as I father'd! Tom, away!
Mark the high noises;[299] and thyself bewray,
When false opinion, whose wrong thought defiles thee,
In thy just proof, repeals and reconciles thee.
What will hap more to-night,[300] safe 'scape the King!
Lurk, lurk. [*Exit.*]

---

[297] *Convenience* is here meant as a word of four syllables, and must be so in order to fill up the verse. In like manner, the Poet repeatedly uses *conscience* and *patience* as trisyllables. Generally, indeed, in Shakespeare's time, the ending *-ience* was used by the poets as two syllables or as one, according to the occasion of their verse.

[298] That is, *can hardly be cured.* Similarly a little before: "Stand in assured loss." And a like phrase occurs in *Othello*, ii. 1: "Therefore my hopes, riot suffocate to death, *stand in bold cure.*"

[299] The great events that are at hand; the exciting sounds of war.

[300] The meaning is, "*Whatsoever* else may happen to-night."

Scene VII.

A Room in GLOUCESTER's *Castle.*

[*Enter* CORNWALL, REGAN, GONERIL, EDMUND, *and* SERVANTS.]

CORNWALL. Post speedily to my lord your husband; show him this letter: the army of France is landed.—Seek out the villain Gloucester. [*Exeunt some of the* SERVANTS.]

REGAN. Hang him instantly.

GONERIL. Pluck out his eyes.

CORNWALL. Leave him to my displeasure.—Edmund, keep you our sister company: the revenges we are bound to take upon your traitorous father are not fit for your beholding. Advise the duke, where you are going, to a most festinate[301] preparation: we are bound to the like. Our posts shall be swift and intelligent betwixt us.—Farewell, dear sister;—farewell, my Lord of Gloucester.[302]—

[*Enter* OSWALD.]

How now! where's the King?

OSWALD. My lord of Gloucester hath convey'd him hence:
Some five or six and thirty of his knights,
Hot questrists[303] after him, met him at gate;
Who, with some other of the lords dependants,[304]
Are gone with him towards Dover; where they boast
To have well-armed friends.

CORNWALL. Get horses for your mistress.

GONERIL. Farewell, sweet lord, and sister.

CORNWALL. Edmund, farewell.—

[*Exeunt* GONERIL, EDMUND, *and* OSWALD.]

Go seek the traitor Gloucester,
Pinion him like a thief, bring him before us.

---

[301] *Festinate* is *speedy.* Not used again by the Poet, though he has *festinately* in the same sense.

[302] Meaning Edmund, who is now invested with his father's titles. Oswald, speaking immediately after, refers to the father by the same title.

[303] *Questrists* for *pursuers*; those who go in *quest* of any thing.

[304] These are probably lords dependent on the Earl of Gloster. I formerly thought them to be some of the King's proper retinue; but Mr. Furness gives such reasons for thinking otherwise, that I gladly stand corrected.

[*Exeunt other* SERVANTS.]

Though well we may not pass[305] upon his life
Without the form of justice, yet our power
Shall do a courtesy to our wrath,[306] which men
May blame, but not control.—Who's there? the traitor?

[*Enter* GLOUCESTER, *brought in by two or three.*]

REGAN. Ingrateful fox! 'tis he.
CORNWALL. Bind fast his corky[307] arms.
GLOUCESTER. What mean your graces? Good my friends, consider
    You are my guests: do me no foul play, friends.
CORNWALL. Bind him, I say. [SERVANTS *bind him.*]
REGAN. Hard, hard.—O filthy traitor!
GLOUCESTER. Unmerciful lady as you are, I'm none.
CORNWALL. To this chair bind him.—Villain, thou shalt find—

[REGAN *plucks his beard.*]

GLOUCESTER. By the kind gods, 'tis most ignobly done
    To pluck me by the beard.
REGAN. So white, and such a traitor!
GLOUCESTER. Naughty lady,
    These hairs, which thou dost ravish from my chin,
    Will quicken,[308] and accuse thee: I am your host:
    With robbers' hands my hospitable favours[309]
    You should not ruffle thus. What will you do?
CORNWALL. Come, sir, what letters had you late from France?
REGAN. Be simple answerer, for we know the truth.
CORNWALL. And what confederacy have you with the traitors
    Late footed in the kingdom?
REGAN. To whose hands have you sent the lunatic King? Speak.
GLOUCESTER. I have a letter guessingly set down,
    Which came from one that's of a neutral heart,
    And not from one opposed.
CORNWALL. Cunning.
REGAN. And false.
CORNWALL. Where hast thou sent the King?

---

[305] That is, pass *sentence* or *judgment*. To *pass* was often used thus.
[306] Shall *bend* to our wrath; *wait upon* it or be its servant.
[307] *Corky* means *dry, withered*, or *shrivelled* with age.
[308] That is, will *become alive*, or assume *life*. The old sense of *quick*.
[309] Here, as often, *favours* is *features*.

GLOUCESTER. To Dover.

REGAN. Wherefore to Dover? Wast thou not charged at peril—

CORNWALL. Wherefore to Dover?—Let him first answer that.

GLOUCESTER. I am tied to the stake, and I must stand the course.[310]

REGAN. Wherefore to Dover, sir?

GLOUCESTER. Because I would not see thy cruel nails
    Pluck out his poor old eyes; nor thy fierce sister
    In his anointed flesh stick boarish fangs.
    The sea, with such a storm as his bare head
    In Hell-black night endured, would have buoy'd up,
    And quench'd the stelled fires:[311] yet, poor old heart,
    He holp the Heavens to rain.
    If wolves had at thy gate howl'd that stern time,
    Thou shouldst have said *Good porter, turn the key*,
    All cruels else subscribed: but I shall see
    The winged vengeance overtake such children.[312]

CORNWALL. See't shalt thou never. Fellows, hold the chair.
    Upon these eyes of thine I'll set my foot.

GLOUCESTER. He that will think to live till he be old,
    Give me some help!—O cruel! O you gods!

REGAN. One side will mock another; the other too.

CORNWALL. If you see vengeance,—

FIRST SERVANT. Hold your hand, my lord:
    I have served you ever since I was a child;
    But better service have I never done you
    Than now to bid you hold.

REGAN. How now, you dog!

FIRST SERVANT. If you did wear a beard upon your chin,
    I'd shake it on this quarrel. What do you mean?

CORNWALL. My villain! [*Draws.*]

FIRST SERVANT. Nay, then, come on, and take the chance of anger.

[*Draws. They fight.* CORNWALL *is wounded.*]

---

[310] An allusion to bear-baiting, where the custom was to chain a bear to a post, and then set the dogs on him.

[311] "The *stellèd* fires" are the *starry* lights; *stella* being the Latin for *star*.—Heath says, "The verb *buoy up* is here used as a verb deponent, or as the middle form of the Greek verbs, to signify *buoy* or *lift itself up.*"

[312] *Cruels*, probably, for *cruelties*, or *acts of cruelty*; *subscribe* an imperative verb, with *cruels* for its object; and *but* with the force of *if not*, like the Latin *nisi*. So that the meaning probably is, "Subscribe thou, that is, underwrite, guarantee, make good, all other deeds or instances of cruelty, if I do not see," &c. In other words, "If swift retribution be not seen to catch you for what you have done, then do not scruple to go security, to stand sponsor for all possible strains of inhumanity." The Poet has many words shortened in like manner; as *dispose* for *disposition, suspects* for *suspicious, characts* for *characters*, &c. He also has many instances of *but* used in that way. So in *Othello*, iii. 3: "Perdition catch my soul, *but* I do love thee!"

REGAN. Give me thy sword.—A peasant stand up thus!

[*Seizes a sword, and runs at him behind.*]

FIRST SERVANT. O, I am slain! My lord, you have one eye left
　　To see some mischief on him.—O! [*Dies.*]
CORNWALL. Lest it see more, prevent it. Out, vile jelly!
　　Where is thy lustre now?[313]
GLOUCESTER. All dark and comfortless. Where's my son Edmund?
　　Edmund, enkindle all the sparks of nature,
　　To quit[314] this horrid act.
REGAN. Out, treacherous villain!
　　Thou call'st on him that hates thee: it was he
　　That made the overture[315] of thy treasons to us;
　　Who is too good to pity thee.
GLOUCESTER. O my follies!
　　Then Edgar was abused.—
　　Kind gods, forgive me that, and prosper him!
REGAN. Go thrust him out at gates, and let him smell
　　His way to Dover.—How is't, my lord? how look you?
CORNWALL. I have received a hurt: follow me, lady.—
　　Turn out that eyeless villain; throw this slave
　　Upon the dunghill.—Regan, I bleed apace:
　　Untimely comes this hurt: give me your arm.

[*Exit* CORNWALL, *led by* REGAN—*Some of the* SERVANTS
　　unbind GLOSTER, *and lead him out.*]

SECOND SERVANT. I'll never care what wickedness I do,
　　If this man come to good.
THIRD SERVANT. If she live long,
　　And in the end meet the old course of death,

---

[313] The shocking savagery here displayed is commented on by Coleridge thus: "I will not disguise my conviction that, in this one point, the tragic in this play has been urged beyond the outermost mark and *ne plus ultra* of the dramatic." And again: "What shall I say of this scene? There is my reluctance to think Shakespeare wrong, and yet—" Professor Dowden remarks as follows: "The treachery of Edmund, and the torture to which Gloster is subjected, are out of the course of familiar experience; but they are commonplace and prosaic in comparison with the inhumanity of the sisters, and the agony of Lear. When we have climbed the steep ascent of Gloster's mount of passion, we see still above us another *via dolorosa* leading to that 'wall of eagle-baffling mountain, black, wintry, dead, unmeasured,' to which Lear is chained. Thus the one story of horror serves as a means of approach to the other, and helps us to conceive its magnitude."

[314] *Quit* for *requite* is very frequent in Shakespeare.

[315] *Overture*, here, is *revealment* or *disclosure*.

Women will all turn monsters.[316]

SECOND SERVANT. Let's follow the old earl, and get the Bedlam
    To lead him where he would: his roguish madness
    Allows itself to any thing.
THIRD SERVANT. Go thou: I'll fetch some flax and whites of eggs
    To apply to his bleeding face. Now, Heaven help him!

[*Exeunt severally.*]

ACT IV.

SCENE I.

The Heath.

[*Enter* EDGAR.]

EDGAR. Yet better thus, and known to be contemn'd,
    Than still contemn'd and flatter'd. To be worst,
    The lowest and most dejected thing of fortune,[317]
    Stands still in esperance,[318] lives not in fear:
    The lamentable change is from the best;
    The worst returns to laughter.[319] Welcome, then,
    Thou unsubstantial air that I embrace!
    The wretch that thou hast blown unto the worst
    Owes nothing to thy blasts.[320] But who comes here?

[*Enter* GLOUCESTER, *led by an* OLD MAN.]

My father, poorly led?—World, world, O world!
But that thy strange mutations make us hate thee,
Lie would not yield to age.[321]

---

[316] The Poet might have justified the act by the supposed barbarity of the legendary age whose manners he was tracing, and urged that their familiarity with such acts prevented the actors in them from recognizing the horrible. No such thing. By inserting in the group a servant who *did* recognize its intrinsic horror, and compassionated the sufferer, he converted disgust into pity. The valiant menial revenges on the spot the wrong done to humanity. The other servants also compassionate the blind old man, to lead him out, to help him, to heal his wounds, and to place him in safe custody. The entire current of feeling is turned in the direction of pity by the force of sympathy. Thus the horror in the 'horrid act' is mitigated, and reduced to the level of terror.—HERAUD.

[317] "Dejected thing of fortune" is thing *cast down by* fortune.

[318] *Esperance* is *hope*; from the French. Used repeatedly by the Poet.

[319] Because, when the worst has come, there can be no further change but for the better. *Laughter* is an instance of the effect put for the cause.

[320] Is not indebted to thy blasts for any favour shown him: they have done their worst upon him, and so absolved him from all obligations."

OLD MAN. O, my good lord, I have been your tenant, and your
    father's tenant, these fourscore years.
GLOUCESTER. Away, get thee away; good friend, be gone:
    Thy comforts can do me no good at all;
    Thee they may hurt.
OLD MAN. Alack, sir, you cannot see your way.
GLOUCESTER. I have no way, and therefore want no eyes;
    I stumbled when I saw: full oft 'tis seen,
    Our maims secure us, and our mere[322] defects
    Prove our commodities.—O dear son Edgar,
    The food of thy abused[323] father's wrath!
    Might I but live to see thee in my touch,
    I'd say I had eyes again!
OLD MAN. How now! Who's there?
EDGAR. [*Aside.*] O gods! Who is't can say *I am at the worst?*
    I am worse than e'er I was.
OLD MAN. 'Tis poor mad Tom.
EDGAR. [*Aside.*] And worse I may be yet: the worst is not
    So long as we can say *This is the worst.*[324]
OLD MAN. Fellow, where goest?
GLOUCESTER. Is it a beggar-man?
OLD MAN. Madman and beggar too.
GLOUCESTER. He has some reason, else he could not beg.
    I' the last night's storm I such a fellow saw;
    Which made me think a man a worm: my son
    Came then into my mind;[325] and yet my mind
    Was then scarce friends with him: I have heard more since.
    As flies to wanton boys, are we to the gods.
    They kill us for their sport.
EDGAR. [*Aside.*] How should this be?
    Bad is the trade that must play Fool to sorrow,
    Angering itself and others.[326]—Bless thee, master!

---

    [321] The meaning seems to be, "Did not thy calamitous reverses make life a burden, old age would never be reconciled or resigned to death."

    [322] Shakespeare repeatedly has *very* in the sense of *mere*: here he has *mere* in the sense of *very.*—*Maim* was often used for any defect, blemish, or imperfection, whether "in mind, body, or estate." So Hooker, *Ecclesiastical Polity*, Book V., Sect. 65: "If men of so good experience and insight in the *maims* of our weak flesh, have thought," &c. Also, Sect. 2.4.: "In a minister ignorance and disability to teach is a *maim.*"

    [323] *Abused* for *deceived* or *deluded.* A frequent usage.

    [324] Because we must still be living, else we could not speak. Edgar at first thinks his condition already as bad as it can be: then the sight of his eyeless father adds a further woe; and now he concludes death to be the worst.

    [325] This remembrance without recognition is a delectable touch of nature. Shakespeare has the same thing in several other cases; particularly the disguised Rosalind in the Forest of Arden, and the disguised Imogen, in *Cymbeline*, v. 5.

    [326] *Angering* in the sense of *grieving*; a common use of *anger* in the Poet's time.

GLOUCESTER. Is that the naked fellow?

OLD MAN. Ay, my lord.

GLOUCESTER. Then, prithee, get thee gone: if, for my sake,
>Thou wilt o'ertake us, hence a mile or twain,
>I' the way toward Dover, do it for ancient love;
>And bring some covering for this naked soul,
>Who I'll entreat to lead me.

OLD MAN. Alack, sir, he is mad.

GLOUCESTER. 'Tis the times' plague, when madmen lead the blind.
>Do as I bid thee, or rather do thy pleasure;
>Above the rest, be gone.[327]

OLD MAN. I'll bring him the best 'parel that I have,
>Come on't what will. [*Exit.*]

GLOUCESTER. Sirrah, naked fellow,—

EDGAR. Poor Tom's a-cold.—[*Aside.*] I cannot daub[328] it further.

GLOUCESTER.—Come hither, fellow.

EDGAR. [*Aside.*] And yet I must.—Bless thy sweet eyes, they bleed.

GLOUCESTER. Know'st thou the way to Dover?

EDGAR. Both stile and gate, horse-way and foot-path. Poor Tom hath been scared out of his good wits: bless thee, good man's son, from the foul fiend! five fiends have been in poor Tom at once; of lust, as Obidicut; Hobbididence, prince of dumbness; Mahu, of stealing; Modo, of murder; Flibbertigibbet, of mopping and mowing, who since possesses chambermaids and waitingwomen.[329] So, bless thee, master!

GLOUCESTER. Here, take this purse, thou whom the Heavens' plagues
>Have humbled to all strokes: that I am wretched
>Makes thee the happier: Heavens, deal so still!
>Let the superfluous[330] and lust-dieted man,

The word is doubtless from the same root, and has the same radical sense, as the Latin *angere*. "*Angaria*," says Richardson, "in Mid-Latin, was used for any vexation, trouble, distress, or anxiety of mind. So *anger*, in our old writers, was applied to any vexation, or distress, or uneasiness of mind or body.—"Playing the Fool to sorrow" means, apparently, acting the Fool's part, to divert off distressing thoughts, or to turn grief into laughter; which may well be painful to both parties. Any attempt to cheer the despondent by forced or affected mirth is apt to have the opposite effect.

[327] This is said because Gloster is anxious for the old man's safety.

[328] To *daub* was sometimes used for to *disguise*. So in *King Richard III.*, iii. 5: "So smooth he *daub'd* his vice with show of virtue." And in like sort the Poet has *daubery* for *imposture*.

[329] "If she have a little helpe of the mother, epilepsie, or cramp, to teach her roll her eyes, wrie her mouth, gnash her teeth, starte with her body, hold her armes and handes stiffe, make antike faces, grinne, *mow and mop* like an ape, then no doubt the young girle is owle-blasted, and *possessed*." So says Harsnet.—To *mop* is to *mock*, to *chatter*; to *mow* is to *make mouths*, to *grimace*.

[330] *Superfluous*, here, probably means *over-clothed*. Gloster is thinking of those who

That slaves your ordinance,[331] that will not see
Because he doth not feel, feel your power quickly;
So distribution should undo excess,
And each man have enough.—Dost thou know Dover?
EDGAR. Ay, master.
GLOUCESTER. There is a cliff, whose high and bending head
Looks fearfully in the confined deep:
Bring me but to the very brim of it,
And I'll repair the misery thou dost bear
With something rich about me: from that place
I shall no leading need.
EDGAR. Give me thy arm:
Poor Tom shall lead thee. [*Exeunt.*]

SCENE II.

Before the Duke of ALBANY'*s Palace.*

[*Enter* GONERIL *and* EDMUND.]

GONERIL. Welcome, my lord:[332] I marvel our mild husband
Not met us on the way.—

[*Enter* OSWALD.]

        Now, where's your master?
OSWALD. Madam, within; but never man so changed.
I told him of the army that was landed;
He smiled at it: I told him you were coming:
His answer was *The worse*: of Gloucester's treachery,
And of the loyal service of his son,
When I inform'd him, then he call'd me sot,
And told me I had turn'd the wrong side out:
What most he should dislike seems pleasant to him;
What like, offensive.
GONERIL. [*To* EDMUND.] Then shall you go no further.
It is the cowish terror of his spirit,

---

live but to eat and drink, and to wear clothes and look fine; thus inverting the just order of
things.
    [331] To *slave* an ordinance is to make it subject to our pleasure, to *be-slave* it, instead
of obeying it as law. So Middleton, in *The Roaring Girl*: "Fortune, who *slaves* men, was
my slave."
    [332] This is in proper sequel to the opening of the last scene of Act iii.: where
Cornwall sends Edmund to escort Goneril home. She is now sweetly welcoming her
escort to her palace, and inviting him to "walk in."

That dares not undertake: he'll not feel wrongs
Which tie him to an answer.[333] Our wishes on the way
May prove effects.[334] Back, Edmund, to my brother;
Hasten his musters and conduct his powers:
I must change arms at home, and give the distaff
Into my husband's hands. This trusty servant
Shall pass between us: ere long you are like to hear,
If you dare venture in your own behalf,
A mistress's command. Wear this; spare speech;

[*Giving a favour.*]

Decline your head:[335] this kiss, if it durst speak,
Would stretch thy spirits up into the air:
Conceive, and fare thee well.
EDMUND. Yours in the ranks of death.
GONERIL. My most dear Gloucester!

[*Exit* EDMUND.]

O, the difference of man and man! To thee
A woman's services are due: my Fool
Usurps my body.
OSWALD. Madam, here comes my lord. [*Exit.*]

[*Enter* ALBANY.]

GONERIL. I have been worth the whistle.[336]
ALBANY. O Goneril!
You are not worth the dust which the rude wind
Blows in your face. I fear your disposition:
That nature, which contemns its origin,
Cannot be border'd certain in itself;[337]

---

[333] The meaning is, that Albany, in his cowardice, *ignores* such wrongs and insults as a man of spirit would energetically resent; thus skulking from danger under a feigned insensibility.

[334] Those wishes of course were, that her ladyship were a widow, or at least free of marriage-bonds. She meditates killing her husband.

[335] She bids him decline his head, that she may give him a kiss, and yet make Oswald believe she is whispering to him. Professor Dowden justly observes that, "to complete the horror they produce in us, these monsters are amorous. Their love is even more hideous than their hate."

[336] Alluding to the proverb, "It is a poor dog that is not *worth the whistling.*" Goneril thinks that her husband, knowing of her coming, ought to have sallied forth, with a retinue, to give her a grand "welcome home."

[337] The meaning is, that the person who has reached such a pitch of unnaturalness as to scorn his parents, and trample on their infirmities, cannot be restrained within any

She that herself will sliver and disbranch
From her material sap, perforce must wither
And come to deadly use.[338]

GONERIL. No more; the text is foolish.

ALBANY. Wisdom and goodness to the vile seem vile:
Filths savour but themselves.[339] What have you done?
Tigers, not daughters, what have you perform'd?
A father, and a gracious aged man,
Whose reverence even the head-lugg'd bear[340] would lick,
Most barbarous, most degenerate! have you madded.
Could my good brother suffer you to do it?
A man, a prince, by him so benefited!
If that the Heavens do not their visible spirits
Send quickly down to tame these vile offences,
It will come,
Humanity must perforce prey on itself,
Like monsters of the deep.[341]

GONERIL. Milk-liver'd man!
That bear'st a cheek for blows, a head for wrongs;
Who hast not in thy brows an eye discerning
Thine honour from thy suffering; that not know'st
Fools do those villains pity who are punish'd
Ere they have done their mischief. Where's thy drum?
France spreads his banners in our noiseless land;
With plumed helm thy slayer begins threats;
Whiles thou, a moral Fool,[342] sit'st still, and criest
Alack, why does he so?

ALBANY. See thyself, devil!
Proper deformity seems not in the fiend

---

certain bounds: there is nothing too bad for him to do. If Goneril will kill her father, whom will she not kill?

[338] "Alluding," says Warburton, "to the use that witches and enchanters are said to make of *withered branches* in their charms. A fine insinuation in the speaker, that she was ready for the most unnatural mischief, and a preparative of the Poet to her plotting with Edmund against her husband's life."—"Come to *deadly* use" is, be put to *fatal* or *destructive* use, as being good only for the Devil to make an instrument of.—"Material sap" is the sap that supplies the *matter* of life, the food.

[339] That is, filths have a taste for nothing but filth, nothing but what is like themselves. "Birds of a feather flock together."

[340] "*Head-lugg'd* bear" probably means a bear made savage by having his head *plucked* or *torn*.

[341] If the gods do not avenge these crimes, the crimes will avenge themselves by turning men into devourers of one another or by inspiring humanity with a rage of self-destruction. A profound truth, and as awful as it is profound! often exemplified, too, in human history.

[342] By "a *moral* fool," this intellectual girl means a *moralizing* fool; one who spins pious yarns about duty, and shirks the offices of manhood.

So horrid as in woman.[343]

GONERIL. O vain Fool!

ALBANY. Thou changed and self-cover'd thing, for shame,
Be-monster not thy feature![344] Were't my fitness
To let these hands obey my blood,
They are apt enough to dislocate and tear
Thy flesh and bones: howe'er[345] thou art a fiend,
A woman's shape doth shield thee.

GONERIL. Marry, your manhood now—

[*Enter a* MESSENGER.]

ALBANY. What news?

MESSENGER. O, my good lord, the Duke of Cornwall's dead:
Slain by his servant, going to put out
The other eye of Gloucester.

ALBANY. Gloucester's eye!

Messenger. A servant that he bred, thrill'd with remorse,[346]
Opposed against the act, bending his sword
To his great master; who, thereat enraged,
Flew on him, and amongst them fell'd him dead;[347]
But not without that harmful stroke, which since
Hath pluck'd him after.

ALBANY. This shows you are above,
You justicers, that these our nether crimes
So speedily can venge!—But, O poor Gloucester!
Lost he his other eye?

MESSENGER. Both, both, my lord.—

---

[343] The deformity, or depravity, of the fiend is proper to him, is his own, and in keeping with the rest of his being, so that the inside and outside agree together; and therefore is less horrid than when it is covered with a woman's shape: for to have the shape of a woman and the heart of a fiend, or to transfuse the inside of the one into the outside of the other, is in the fullest sense unnatural and monstrous; and she who so translates her inner self literally be-monsters her proper make-up, her womanhood.

[344] *Cover'd* in the sense of *shielded* or *defended*. So that the meaning is the same as "howe'er thou art a fiend, a *woman's* shape doth *shield* thee."—*Changed* is *transformed*. Albany seems to regard his wife as having *disnatured* her inner self from what he had seen or supposed her to be.—Here, as in one or two other places, feature seems to have very much the sense of its Latin original, *facere*, and so to stand for *nature, make, self-hood*, or *constitutive propriety*, as *set forth in the preceding note*. As Goneril is well endowed with formal beauty, her moral deformity, or her be-devilled inside, only renders her the more hideous to the inward eye.—For the matter of this note, as also of the preceding, I am indebted to Mr. Joseph Crosby.

[345] *However* has here the force of *although*. Often so.

[346] Here, as usual in Shakespeare, *remorse* is *pity* or *compassion*.

[347] This may seem inconsistent with the matter as represented in a former scene, but it is not really so; for, though Regan thrust the servant with a sword, a wound before received from Cornwall may have caused his death.

This letter, madam, craves a speedy answer;
'Tis from your sister.
GONERIL. [*Aside.*] One way I like this well;
But being widow, and my Gloucester with her,
May all the building in my fancy pluck
Upon my hateful life:[348] another way,
The news is not so tart.—I'll read, and answer. [*Exit.*]
ALBANY. Where was his son when they did take his eyes?
MESSENGER. Come with my lady hither.
ALBANY. He is not here.
MESSENGER. No, my good lord; I met him back again.
ALBANY. Knows he the wickedness?
MESSENGER. Ay, my good lord; 'twas he inform'd against him;
And quit the house on purpose, that their punishment
Might have the freer course.
ALBANY. Gloucester, I live
To thank thee for the love thou show'dst the King,
And to revenge thine eyes.—Come hither, friend:
Tell me what more thou know'st. [*Exeunt.*]

SCENE III.

The French Camp near Dover.

[*Enter* KENT *and a* GENTLEMAN.[349]]

KENT. Why the King of France is so suddenly gone back know you
    the reason?
GENTLEMAN. Something he left imperfect in the state, which since
    his coming forth is thought of; which imports to the kingdom so
    much fear and danger, that his personal return was most required
    and necessary.
KENT. Who hath he left behind him general?
GENTLEMAN. The Marshal of France, Monsieur La Far.
KENT. Did your letters pierce the queen to any demonstration of grief?
GENTLEMAN. Ay, sir; she took them, read them in my presence;
    And now and then an ample tear trill'd down

---

[348] Goneril likes this well, inasmuch as she has now but to make away with her
sister and her husband by poison, and then the whole kingdom will be hers to share with
Edmund, whom she intends to marry: but, on the other hand, Regan, being now a widow,
and having Edmund with her, may win him by holding out a more practicable match; and
so the castle which Goneril has built in imagination may rush down upon her own head.
"Building *in* my fancy" for building of my fancy.

[349] This is the same Gentleman whom in a previous scene Kent dispatched to Dover,
with letters for Cordelia. See page 72, note 224.

Her delicate cheek: it seem'd she was a queen
Over her passion; who, most rebel-like,
Sought to be King o'er her.
KENT. O, then it moved her.
GENTLEMAN. Not to a rage: patience and sorrow strove
  Who should express her goodliest. You have seen
  Sunshine and rain at once: her smiles and tears
  Were like a better way,[350]—those happy smilets,
  That play'd on her ripe lip, seem'd not to know
  What guests were in her eyes; which parted thence,
  As pearls from diamonds dropp'd. In brief,
  Sorrow would be a rarity most beloved,
  If all could so become it.
KENT. Made she no verbal question?[351]
GENTLEMAN. Faith, once or twice she heaved the name of *father*
  Pantingly forth, as if it press'd her heart:
  Cried, *Sisters! sisters! Shame of ladies! sisters!*
  Kent! father! sisters! What, i' the storm? i' the night?
  Let pity not be believed! There she shook
  The holy water from her heavenly eyes,
  And clamour moisten'd,[352] then away she started
  To deal with grief alone.
KENT. It is the stars,
  The stars above us, govern our conditions;[353]
  Else one self mate and mate could not beget
  Such different issues. You spoke not with her since?
GENTLEMAN. No.
KENT. Was this before the King return'd?
GENTLEMAN. No, since.
KENT. Well, sir, the poor distressed Lear's i' the town;
  Who sometime, in his better tune, remembers
  What we are come about, and by no means
  Will yield to see his daughter.
GENTLEMAN. Why, good sir?
KENT. A sovereign shame so elbows him:[354] his own unkindness,

---

[350] That is, her smiles and tears were like sunshine and rain at once; the sense being completed at *like*. He then proceeds to say the same thing again, in what he regards as "a better way."—*Smilets* is a diminutive of *smiles: semi-smiles* is nearly the force of it.

[351] *Question* for *expression* or *utterance*. It is often met with in the kindred sense of *talk* or *conversation*.

[352] An odd and not very happy expression; but meaning, apparently, that she wept aloud, or that her crying was drenched with tears.

[353] *Condition*, as usual, for *temper* or *disposition*. As Cordelia and her sisters had the same father and mother, Kent can only account for the difference in them by the effects of "spherical predominance."

[354] There has been some strange stumbling at this innocent expression. I take the

That stripp'd her from his benediction, turn'd her
To foreign casualties, gave her dear rights
To his dog-hearted daughters,—these things sting
His mind so venomously, that burning shame
Detains him from Cordelia.
GENTLEMAN. Alack, poor gentleman!
KENT. Of Albany's and Cornwall's powers you heard not?
GENTLEMAN. 'Tis so, they are afoot.
KENT. Well, sir, I'll bring you to our master Lear,
And leave you to attend him: some dear cause
Will in concealment wrap me up awhile;
When I am known aright, you shall not grieve
Lending me this acquaintance. I pray you, go
Along with me. [*Exeunt.*]

SCENE IV.

The Same. A tent.

[*Enter* CORDELIA, *a* DOCTOR, *and* SOLDIERS.]

CORDELIA. Alack, 'tis he: why, he was met even now
As mad as the vex'd sea; singing aloud;
Crown'd with rank femiter and furrow-weeds,
With bur-docks, hemlock, nettles, cuckoo-flowers,
Darnel, and all the idle weeds that grow
In our sustaining corn.[355]—A century send forth;
Search every acre in the high-grown field,
And bring him to our eye. [*Exit an* OFFICER.]—What can man's
   wisdom
In the restoring his bereaved sense?
He that helps him take all my outward worth.
DOCTOR. There is means, madam:
Our foster-nurse of nature is repose,
The which he lacks; that to provoke in him,
Are many simples[356] operative, whose power

---

meaning to be, a *predominant* shame so *digs him in the side.* And why not such a metaphor, to express the action of shame?

[355] Called *sustaining,* probably because it sustains or feeds us, and so makes an apt antithesis to *idle weeds,*—*idle* as being *useless.*—A *century* is, properly, a troop of a *hundred* men. Hence the commander of such a troop was called a *centurion.*

[356] *Simples* properly meant medicinal *herbs,* but was used for *medicines* in general.—Upon this remarkable passage Dr. A. O. Kellogg comments as follows: "This reply is significant, and worthy of careful attention, as embracing a brief summary of almost the only true principles recognized by modern science, and now carried out by the most eminent physicians in the treatment of the insane."

Will close the eye of anguish.
CORDELIA. All blest secrets,
    All you unpublish'd virtues of the earth,
    Spring with my tears! be aidant and remediate
    In the good man's distress!—Seek, seek for him;
    Lest his ungovern'd rage dissolve the life
    That wants the means to lead it.

[*Enter a* MESSENGER.]

MESSENGER. News, madam;
    The British powers are marching hitherward.
CORDELIA. 'Tis known before; our preparation stands
    In expectation of them.—O dear father,
    It is thy business that I go about;
    Therefore great France
    My mourning and important[357] tears hath pitied.
    No blown[358] ambition doth our arms incite,
    But love, dear love, and our aged father's right:
    Soon may I hear and see him! [*Exeunt.*]

SCENE V.

A Room in GLOUCESTER's *Castle.*

[*Enter* REGAN *and* OSWALD.]

REGAN. But are my brother's powers set forth?
OSWALD. Ay, madam.
REGAN. Himself in person there?
OSWALD. Madam, with much ado:
    Your sister is the better soldier.
REGAN. Lord Edmund spake not with your lord at home?
OSWALD. No, madam.
REGAN. What might import my sister's letter to him?
OSWALD. I know not, lady.
REGAN. Faith, he is posted hence on serious matter.
    It was great ignorance, Gloucester's eyes being out,
    To let him live: where he arrives he moves
    All hearts against us. Edmund, I think, is gone,
    In pity of his misery, to dispatch
    His nighted life; moreover, to descry

---

[357] *Important* for *importunate.*
[358] *Blown*, here, is *swollen, inflated, puffed.*

The strength o' the enemy.

OSWALD. I must needs after him, madam, with my letter.

REGAN. Our troops set forth to-morrow: stay with us;
    The ways are dangerous.

OSWALD. I may not, madam:
    My lady charged my duty in this business.

REGAN. Why should she write to Edmund? Might not you
    Transport her purposes by word? Belike,
    Something—I know not what: I'll love thee much,
    Let me unseal the letter.

OSWALD. Madam, I had rather—

REGAN. I know your lady does not love her husband;
    I am sure of that: and at her late being here
    She gave strange oeillades[359] and most speaking looks
    To noble Edmund. I know you are of her bosom.[360]

OSWALD. I, madam?

REGAN. I speak in understanding; you are; I know't:
    Therefore I do advise you, take this note:[361]
    My lord is dead; Edmund and I have talk'd;
    And more convenient is he for my hand
    Than for your lady's: you may gather more.[362]
    If you do find him, pray you, give him this;[363]
    And when your mistress hears thus much from you,
    I pray, desire her call her wisdom to her.[364]
    So, fare you well.
    If you do chance to hear of that blind traitor,
    Preferment[365] falls on him that cuts him off.

OSWALD. Would I could meet him, madam! I should show
    What party I do follow.

REGAN. Fare thee well. [*Exeunt.*]

---

[359] *Eye-glances.* Cotgrave's *French Dictionary:* "Oeillade: An amorous looke, affectionate wink, wanton aspect, or passionate cast of the eye."

[360] In her *confidence*; or, as we should say, her bosom confidant.

[361] "Take note, or knowledge, of this." See page 72, note 224.

[362] "You may infer more than I have told you."

[363] Probably handing him a ring or some token for Edmund.

[364] Regan's cold, penetrating virulence is well shown in this. The plain English of it is, "Tell her to do her worst, and help herself, if she can."

[365] *Preferment* for *promotion* or *advancement.* Repeatedly so.

SCENE VI.

The Country near Dover.

[*Enter* GLOUCESTER, *and* EDGAR *dressed like a Peasant.*]

GLOUCESTER. When shall we come to th' top of that same hill?
EDGAR. You do climb up it now: look, how we labour.
GLOUCESTER. Methinks the ground is even.
EDGAR. Horrible steep.
    Hark, do you hear the sea?
GLOUCESTER. No, truly.
EDGAR. Why, then, your other senses grow imperfect
    By your eyes' anguish.
GLOUCESTER. So may it be, indeed:
    Methinks thy voice is alter'd; and thou speak'st
    In better phrase and matter than thou didst.
EDGAR. You're much deceived: in nothing am I changed
    But in my garments.
GLOUCESTER. Methinks you're better spoken.
EDGAR. Come on, sir; here's the place: stand still. How fearful
    And dizzy 'tis, to cast one's eyes so low!
    The crows and choughs that wing the midway air
    Show scarce so gross as beetles: half way down
    Hangs one that gathers samphire,[366] dreadful trade!
    Methinks he seems no bigger than his head:
    The fishermen, that walk upon the beach,
    Appear like mice; and yond tall anchoring bark,
    Diminish'd to her cock;[367] her cock, a buoy
    Almost too small for sight: the murmuring surge,
    That on the unnumber'd[368] idle pebbles chafes,
    Cannot be heard so high. I'll look no more;
    Lest my brain turn, and the deficient sight
    Topple down headlong.
GLOUCESTER. Set me where you stand.
EDGAR. Give me your hand: you are now within a foot

---

[366] In Shakespeare's time the cliffs of Dover were noted for the production of this plant. It is thus spoken of in Smith's *History of Waterford*, 1774: "Samphire grows in great plenty on most of the sea-cliffs in this country. It is terrible to see how people gather it, *hanging by a rope* several fathom from the top of the impending rocks, as it were in the air." It was made into a pickle and eaten as a relish.

[367] That is, her *cock-boat.* Hence the term *cock-swain.*

[368] *Unnumber'd* for *innumerable*; a frequent usage in old writers, and not without examples now. See page 45, note 109.

Of the extreme verge: for all beneath the moon
Would I not leap upright.[369]
GLOUCESTER. Let go my hand.

Here, friend, 's another purse; in it a jewel
Well worth a poor man's taking: fairies and gods
Prosper it with thee! Go thou farther off;
Bid me farewell, and let me hear thee going.

EDGAR. Now fare you well, good sir.
GLOUCESTER. With all my heart.
EDGAR. [*Aside.*] Why I do trifle thus with his despair
Is done to cure it.
GLOUCESTER. [*Kneeling.*] O you mighty gods!

This world I do renounce, and, in your sights,
Shake patiently my great affliction off:
If I could bear it longer, and not fall
To quarrel with your great opposeless wills,
My snuff and loathed part of nature should
Burn itself out. If Edgar live, O, bless him!—
Now, fellow, fare thee well.

EDGAR. Gone, sir: farewell.—

[GLOUCESTER *throws himself forward, and falls.*]

[*Aside.*] And yet I know not how conceit may rob
The treasury of life,[370] when life itself
Yields to the theft: had he been where he thought,
By this, had thought been past.—Alive or dead?
Ho, you sir! friend! Hear you, sir! speak!
[*Aside.*] Thus might he pass indeed: yet he revives.—
What are you, sir?

GLOUCESTER. Away, and let me die.
EDGAR. Hadst thou been aught but gossamer,[371] feathers, air,

---

[369] Heath's explanation is probably right: "This expression was purposely intended to heighten the horror of the description, and to affect the reader's imagination the more strongly. The spot is therefore represented as so extremely near the edge of the precipice, that there was the utmost hazard in leaping even upright upon it."

[370] *Conceit* in its old sense of *conception* or *imagination.*—*How* must here be taken as equivalent to *whether* or *but that.* So that the meaning comes something thus: "When one is thus longing to die, I do not know but that the mere imagination of such a leap, or such a fall, might be the death of him." This accords with what Edgar says a little after: "Thus might he pass indeed." So in the Poet's dedication of his *Venus and Adonis* to the Earl of Southampton: "I know not *how* I shall offend in dedicating my unpolished lines to your lordship."

[371] The substance called *gossamer* is formed of the collected webs of spiders. Some think it the down of plants; others the vapour arising from boggy or marshy ground in warm weather. The etymon of this word is said to be *summer goose* or *summer gauze*, hence "gauze o' the summer."

So many fathom down precipitating,
Thou'dst shiver'd like an egg: but thou dost breathe;
Hast heavy substance; bleed'st not; speak'st; art sound.
Ten masts at each[372] make not the altitude
Which thou hast perpendicularly fell:
Thy life's a miracle. Speak yet again.

GLOUCESTER. But have I fall'n, or no?

EDGAR. From the dread summit of this chalky bourn.
Look up a-height; the shrill-gorged[373] lark so far
Cannot be seen or heard: do but look up.

GLOUCESTER. Alack, I have no eyes.
Is wretchedness deprived that benefit,
To end itself by death? 'Twas yet some comfort,
When misery could beguile the tyrant's rage,
And frustrate his proud will.

EDGAR. Give me your arm:
Up: so. How is't? Feel you your legs? You stand.

GLOUCESTER. Too well, too well.

EDGAR. This is above all strangeness.
Upon the crown o' the cliff, what thing was that
Which parted from you?

GLOUCESTER. A poor unfortunate beggar.

EDGAR. As I stood here below, methought his eyes
Were two full moons; he had a thousand noses,
Horns whelk'd and waved like the enridged sea.[374]
It was some fiend; therefore, thou happy father,
Think that the clearest gods, who make them honours
Of men's impossibilities,[375] have preserved thee.

GLOUCESTER. I do remember now: henceforth I'll bear
Affliction till it do cry out itself
Enough, enough, and die. That thing you speak of,
I took it for a man; often 'twould say
The fiend, the fiend! he led me to that place.

---

[372] A strange expression, but meaning, perhaps, ten masts *joined each to the other*, or *drawn out* in length. This explanation may be justified by observing that *each* is from the Anglo-Saxon *eacan*, to *add*, to *augment*, or *lengthen*. *Eke*, sometimes spelt *eche*, is from the same source.

[373] *Shrill* is loud, as in *Julius Caesar*, i. 2: "I hear a tongue, *shriller* than all the music, cry *Caesar!*" "Shrill-*gorged*" is *loud-throated*, or *loud-voiced*.

[374] *Whelk'd* is marked with protuberances. The *whelk* is a small shellfish, so called, perhaps, because its shell is marked with convolved protuberant ridges.—The sea is *enridged* when blown into *waves*.

[375] *Men's impossibilities* are things that seem to men impossible.—The incident of Gloster being made to believe himself ascending, and leaping from, the chalky cliff has always struck me as a very notable case of inherent improbability overcome in effect by opulence of description.

EDGAR. Bear free and patient thoughts.—But who comes here?

[*Enter* KING LEAR, *fantastically dressed with wild flowers.*]

The safer sense will ne'er accommodate
His master thus.[376]

KING LEAR. No, they cannot touch me for coining; I am the King
   himself:—

EDGAR. O thou side-piercing sight!

KING LEAR. Nature's above art in that respect.—There's your press-
   money.[377] That fellow handles his bow like a crow-keeper:[378]—
   draw me a clothier's yard.—Look, look, a mouse! Peace, peace;
   this piece of toasted cheese will do't.—There's my gauntlet; I'll
   prove it on a giant. Bring up the brown bills.—O, well flown,
   bird!—I' the clout, i' the clout: hewgh!—Give the word.[379]

EDGAR. Sweet marjoram.

KING LEAR. Pass.

GLOUCESTER. I know that voice.

KING LEAR. Ha! Goneril,—with a white beard!—They flattered me
   like a dog; and told me I had white hairs in my beard ere the black
   ones were there. To say *ay* and *no* to every thing that I said *ay* and
   no too was no good divinity.[380] When the rain came to wet me
   once, and the wind to make me chatter; when the thunder would
   not peace at my bidding; there I found 'em, there I smelt 'em out.
   Go to, they are not men o' their words: they told me I was every
   thing; 'tis a lie, I am not ague-proof.

GLOUCESTER. The trick[381] of that voice I do well remember:
   Is't not the King?

---

[376] *His* for *its*, referring to *sense*. Edgar is speaking of Lear's *dress*, and judges from
this that he is not in his *safer sense*; that is, in his *senses*.

[377] Lear, I suppose, here imagines himself a recruiting officer, *impressing* men into
the service, and paying them the bounty-money.—The sense of the preceding clause is,
that he, being a king by nature or by birth, is not subject to legal or artificial control
touching the matter in question.

[378] A *crow-keeper* is a thing to keep the crows off the corn; what we call a *scare-
crow*; which was sometimes a figure of a man, with a cross-bow in his hands.—"Draw
me a clothier's yard" means draw me an arrow *the length* of a clothier's yard; the force of
an arrow depending on the length it was drawn in the bow.

[379] The old King is here raving of a challenge, a battle, of falconry, and archery,
jumbled together in quick succession. When he says "There's my gauntlet," he is a
champion throwing down his glove by way of challenge. When he says "Give the word,"
he is a sentinel on guard, demanding the watchword or countersign. *Brown bill* is an old
term for a kind of *battle-axe*; here put for men armed with that weapon. *Well flown, bird,*
was the falconer's expression when the hawk made a good flight. *The clout* is the *white
mark* at which archers aim.

[380] To tie our assent and dissent entirely to another, to speak nothing but in echo of
his *yes* and *no*, is the extreme of sycophancy; and may well be called "no good divinity."

[381] *Trick* for *peculiarity* or *characteristic*.

KING LEAR. Ay, every inch a King:

> When I do stare, see how the subject quakes.
> I pardon that man's life.—What was thy cause?
> Adultery?
> Thou shalt not die: die for adultery! No:
> The wren goes to't, and the small gilded fly
> Does lecher in my sight.
> Let copulation thrive; for Gloucester's bastard son
> Was kinder to his father than my daughters
> Got 'tween the lawful sheets.
> To't, luxury, pell-mell! for I lack soldiers.
> Behold yond simpering dame,
> Whose face between her forks presages snow;[382]
> That minces virtue,[383] and does shake the head
> To hear of pleasure's name;
> The fitchew, nor the soiled horse[384] goes to't
> With a more riotous appetite.
> Down from the waist they are Centaurs,
> Though women all above:
> But to the girdle do the gods inherit,[385]
> Beneath is all the fiends';

> There's Hell, there's darkness, there's the sulphurous pit, Burning,
> scalding, stench, consumption; fie, fie, fie! pah, pah!—Give me an
> ounce of civet,[386] good apothecary, to sweeten my imagination:
> there's money for thee.

GLOUCESTER. O, let me kiss that hand!

KING LEAR. Let me wipe it first; it smells of mortality.

GLOUCESTER. O ruin'd piece of nature! This great world
> Shall so wear out to nought.—Dost thou know me?

---

[382] The order, according to the sense, is, "Whose face presages snow between her forks." The same thought is imaged with more delicacy in *Timon*, iv. 3: "Whose blush doth thaw the consecrated snow that lies on Dian's lap."

[383] That affects or puts on the coyness or modesty of virtue. Cotgrave explains *mineux-se*, "*Outward seeming*, also squeamish, quaint, coy, that *minces it* exceedingly."

[384] The *fitchew* is the *pole-cat*.—*Soiled* is well explained by Heath: "A horse is said to be soiled when, after having been long stalled, he is turned out for a few weeks in the Spring, to take the first flush of the new grass, which both cleanses him and fills him with blood."

[385] *Inherit* in its old sense of *possess*.

[386] *Civet* is the old name of a musky perfume; obtained from what is called the civet-cat. So, in iii. 4, Lear says to Edgar, "Thou owest the worm no silk, the *cat* no *perfume*."

KING LEAR. I remember thine eyes well enough. Dost thou squiny at me? No, do thy worst, blind Cupid! I'll not love. Read thou this challenge; mark but the penning of it.

GLOUCESTER. Were all the letters suns, I could not see one.

EDGAR. [*Aside.*] I would not take this from report; it is,
And my heart breaks at it.

KING LEAR. Read.

GLOUCESTER. What, with the case of eyes?

KING LEAR. O, ho, are you there with me?[387] No eyes in your head, nor no money in your purse? Your eyes are in a heavy case, your purse in a light; yet you see how this world goes.

GLOUCESTER. I see it feelingly.

KING LEAR. What, art mad? A man may see how this world goes with no eyes. Look with thine ears: see how yond justice rails upon yond simple thief. Hark, in thine ear: change places; and, handy-dandy,[388] which is the justice, which is the thief? Thou hast seen a farmer's dog bark at a beggar?

GLOUCESTER. Ay, sir.

KING LEAR. And the creature run from the cur? There thou mightst behold the great image of authority: a dog's obeyed in office.—

> Thou rascal beadle, hold thy bloody hand!
> Why dost thou lash that whore? Strip thine own back;
> Thou hotly lust'st to use her in that kind
> For which thou whipp'st her. The usurer hangs the cozener.[389]
> Through tatter'd clothes small vices do appear;
> Robes and furr'd gowns hide all. Plate sin with gold,
> And the strong lance of justice hurtless breaks:
> Arm it in rags, a pigmy's straw does pierce it.
> None does offend, none, I say, none; I'll able 'em:[390]
> Take that of me, my friend, who have the power
> To seal the accuser's lips.—Get thee glass eyes;
> And like a scurvy politician, seem
> To see the things thou dost not.—Now, now, now, now:
> Pull off my boots: harder, harder: so.

---

[387] That is, "is that what you mean?" A like instance occurs in *As You Like It*, v. 2: "O, I know where you are": *where you are* for *what you mean.* So, in old language, to *go along with* one is to *understand* him.

[388] *Handy-dandy* is an old game of children; one child enclosing something in his hand, and using a sort of legerdemain, changing it swiftly from hand to hand, and then calling upon his playfellow to guess which hand it is in; the latter to have the thing, if he guesses right.

[389] *Cozener* and to *cozen* were much used in the Poet's time, and are not entirely out of use yet. To *cozen* is to *cheat*, to *swindle*.

[390] The meaning is, "I will *cancel* their *disability*"; or, "I will *warrant* or *answer for* them."

EDGAR. O, matter and impertinency mix'd![391]
    Reason in madness!
KING LEAR. If thou wilt weep my fortunes, take my eyes.
    I know thee well enough; thy name is Gloucester:
    Thou must be patient; we came crying hither:
    Thou know'st, the first time that we smell the air,
    We waul and cry.[392] I will preach to thee: mark.
GLOUCESTER. Alack, alack the day!
KING LEAR. When we are born, we cry that we are come
    To this great stage of fools.—'Tis a good block;
    It were a delicate stratagem, to shoe
    A troop of horse with felt:[393] I'll put't in proof;
    And when I have stol'n upon these sons-in-law,
    Then, kill, kill, kill, kill, kill, kill![394]

    [*Enter a* GENTLEMAN, *with Attendants.*]

GENTLEMAN. O, here he is: lay hand upon him.—Sir,
    Your most dear daughter—
KING LEAR. No rescue? What, a prisoner? I am even
    The natural Fool of fortune. Use me well;
    You shall have ransom. Let me have surgeons;
    I am cut to th' brains.
GENTLEMAN. You shall have any thing.
KING LEAR. No seconds? all myself?
    Why, this would make a man a man of salt,[395]
    To use his eyes for garden water-pots,
    Ay, and laying Autumn's dust.

---

[391] *Impertinency* in its old sense of *irrelevancy*; that which has no connection with the matter in hand.

[392] This may have been taken from Pliny, as translated by Holland: "Man alone, poor wretch, nature hath laid all naked upon the bare earth, even on his birthday to *cry* and *wrawle* presently from the very first houre that he is borne into this world."

[393] So in Fenton's *Tragical Discourses*, 1567: "He attyreth himself for the purpose in a night-gowne girt to hym, with a payre of *shoes of felte,* leaste the noyse of his feete might discover his goinge."—When Lear goes to preaching he takes off his hat and holds it in his hand, as preachers were wont to do in the Poet's time. "'Tis a good *block*" doubtless refers to the *shape* or *form* of the *hat*. As he is holding the hat in his hand, or perhaps moulding it into some new shape, the thought strikes him what the hat is made of, and he starts off upon the stratagem of shoeing a troop of horses with *felt*. This use of *block* is well illustrated by a passage in Dekker's *Gull's Hornbook*, 1609: "That cannot observe the tune of his hatband, nor know what fashioned *block* is most kin to his head; for in my opinion the brain cannot chuse his *felt* well."

[394] This was the cry formerly in the English army when an onset was made on the enemy.

[395] Would turn a man all to brine; that is, to *tears.*

GENTLEMAN. Good sir,—

KING LEAR. I will die bravely, like a smug[396] bridegroom. What!
    I will be jovial: come, come; I am a King,
    My masters, know you that.

GENTLEMAN. You are a royal one, and we obey you.

KING LEAR. Then there's life in't.[397] Nay, if you get it, you shall get
    it with running. Sa, sa, sa, sa.[398]

    [*Exit*; ATTENDANTS *follow*.]

GENTLEMAN. A sight most pitiful in the meanest wretch,
    Past speaking of in a King! Thou hast one daughter,
    Who redeems nature from the general curse
    Which twain have brought her to.

EDGAR. Hail, gentle sir.

GENTLEMAN. Sir, speed you: what's your will?

EDGAR. Do you hear aught, sir, of a battle toward?

GENTLEMAN. Most sure and vulgar;[399] every one hears that,
    Which can distinguish sound.

EDGAR. But, by your favour,
    How near's the other army?

GENTLEMAN. Near and on speedy foot; the main descry
    Stands on the hourly thought.[400]

EDGAR. I thank you, sir: that's all.

GENTLEMAN. Though that the queen on special cause is here,
    Her army is moved on.

EDGAR. I thank you, sir. [*Exit* GENTLEMAN.]

GLOUCESTER. You ever-gentle gods, take my breath from me:
    Let not my worser spirit tempt me again
    To die before you please!

EDGAR. Well pray you, father.[401]

GLOUCESTER. Now, good sir, what are you?

EDGAR. A most poor man, made tame to fortune's blows;
    Who, by the art of known and feeling sorrows,
    Am pregnant[402] to good pity. Give me your hand,

---

[396] *Smug* is *spruce, trim, fine.* So in *The Merchant of Venice*, iii. 1: "A beggar, that was used to come so *smug* upon the mart."

[397] There is hope in it yet; the case is not desperate.

[398] These syllables are probably meant for Lear's panting as he runs.

[399] *Vulgar* in its old sense of *common*. A frequent usage.

[400] The main body is expected to be descried every hour.—"On speedy foot" is marching rapidly, or footing it fast.

[401] It was customary for young people to address an aged person as father or mother. Hence Edgar keeps addressing Gloster so without being recognized as his son.

[402] *Pregnant*, here, is *quick, prompt, ready.* Repeatedly so.—*Biding*, in the next line, is *lodging*, or *abiding-place.*

I'll lead you to some biding.
GLOUCESTER. Hearty thanks:
    The bounty and the benison of Heaven
    To boot, and boot!

[*Enter* OSWALD.]

OSWALD. A proclaim'd prize! Most happy!
    That eyeless head of thine was first framed flesh
    To raise my fortunes.—Thou old unhappy traitor,
    Briefly thyself remember:[403] the sword is out
    That must destroy thee.
GLOUCESTER. Now let thy friendly hand
    Put strength enough to't. [EDGAR *interposes.*]
OSWALD. Wherefore, bold peasant,
    Darest thou support a publish'd traitor? Hence;
    Lest that the infection of his fortune take
    Like hold on thee. Let go his arm.
EDGAR. Ch'ill not let go, zir, without vurther 'casion.
OSWALD. Let go, slave, or thou diest!
EDGAR. Good gentleman, go your gait, and let poor volk pass. An chud ha' bin zwaggered out of my life, 'twould not ha' bin zo long as 'tis by a vortnight.[404] Nay, come not near th' old man; keep out, che vor ye, or I'se try whether your costard or my ballow be the harder:[405] ch'ill be plain with you.
OSWALD. Out, dunghill!
EDGAR. Ch'ill pick your teeth, zir: come; no matter vor your foins.[406]

[*They fight, and* EDGAR *knocks him down.*]

OSWALD. Slave, thou hast slain me: villain, take my purse:
    If ever thou wilt thrive, bury my body;
    And give the letters which thou find'st about me
    To Edmund earl of Gloucester; seek him out
    Upon the British party.—O, untimely death! [*Dies.*]
EDGAR. I know thee well: a serviceable villain;
    As duteous to the vices of thy mistress
    As badness would desire.
GLOUCESTER. What, is he dead?

---

[403] "*Quickly* call to mind thy past offences, and repent."

[404] "If I could have been swaggered out of my life, 'twould not have been so long as it is by a fortnight."

[405] "Keep out, *I warn you*, or I'll try whether your head or my *cudgel* be the harder." Edgar here speaks the Somersetshire dialect.

[406] *Foins* are *thrusts*, or passes in fencing. The Poet has the verb to *foin.*

EDGAR. Sit you down, father; rest you
    Let's see these pockets: the letters that he speaks of
    May be my friends. He's dead; I am only sorry
    He had no other death's-man. Let us see:
    Leave, gentle wax; and, manners, blame us not:
    To know our enemies' minds, we'd rip their hearts;
    Their papers, is more lawful.

    [*Reads.*] *Let our reciprocal vows be remember'd. You have many*
    opportunities to cut him off: if your will want not, time and place
    will be fruitfully offered. There is nothing done, if he return the
    conqueror: then am I the prisoner, and his bed my goal; from the
    loathed warmth whereof deliver me, and supply the place for your
    labour.

        Your—wife, so I would say—affectionate servant,
                                    GONERIL.
    O undistinguish'd space of woman's will![407]
    A plot upon her virtuous husband's life;
    And the exchange my brother!—Here, in the sands,
    Thee I'll rake up,[408] the post unsanctified
    Of murderous lechers: and in the mature time
    With this ungracious paper strike the sight
    Of the death practised duke: for him 'tis well
    That of thy death and business I can tell.
GLOUCESTER. The King is mad: how stiff is my vile sense,
    That I stand up, and have ingenious[409] feeling
    Of my huge sorrows! Better I were distract:
    So should my thoughts be sever'd from my griefs,
    And woes by wrong imaginations lose
    The knowledge of themselves.[410]
EDGAR. Give me your hand:

    [*Drum afar off.*]

    Far off, methinks, I hear the beaten drum:
    Come, father, I'll bestow you with a friend. [*Exeunt.*]

---

    [407] *Undistinguish'd* for *indistinguishable*, as, before, *unnumber'd* for *innumerable.*
The meaning probably is, that woman's will has no distinguishable bounds, or no
assignable limits; there is no telling what she will do, or where she will stop.
    [408] That is, "*cover* thee up." Singer says that in Staffordshire to *rake* the fire is to
cover it for the night. So 'tis in New England.
    [409] *Ingenious* is *intelligent, lively, acute.* Warburton says, "*Ingenious feeling*
signifies a feeling from an understanding not disturbed or disordered, but which,
representing things as they are, makes the sense of pain the more exquisite."
    [410] As the woes or sufferings of madmen are lost in imaginary felicities.

SCENE VII.

A Tent in the French camp. LEAR *on a bed asleep, soft music playing;* DOCTOR, GENTLEMAN, *and others attending.*

[*Enter* CORDELIA *and* KENT.]

CORDELIA. O thou good Kent, how shall I live and work,
 To match thy goodness? My life will be too short,
 And every measure fail me.
KENT. To be acknowledged, madam, is o'erpaid.
 All my reports go with the modest truth;
 Nor more nor clipp'd, but so.[411]
CORDELIA. Be better suited:
 These weeds are memories of those worser hours;[412]
 I prithee, put them off.
KENT. Pardon me, dear madam;
 Yet to be known shortens my made intent:[413]
 My boon I make it, that you know me not
 Till time and I think meet.
CORDELIA. Then be't so, my good lord.—[*To the* DOCTOR.]
 How does the King?
DOCTOR. Madam, sleeps still.
CORDELIA. O you kind gods,
 Cure this great breach in his abused nature!
 The untuned and jarring senses, O, wind up
 Of this child-changed father![414]
DOCTOR. So please your majesty
 That we may wake the King: he hath slept long.
CORDELIA. Be govern'd by your knowledge, and proceed
 I' the sway of your own will. Is he array'd?
GENTLEMAN. Ay, madam; in the heaviness of his sleep
 We put fresh garments on him.
DOCTOR. Be by, good madam, when we do awake him;

---

[411] "My reports are neither *exaggerated* nor *curtailed*; neither more nor less than the modest truth."

[412] "Better *suited*" is better *dressed.*—The Poet often has *memory* in the sense of *memorial* or *remembrancer.*

[413] That is, makes or will make me come short of it. Kent's thought is, that the being now known will cause him to fall short, not of his whole purpose, but of what he regards as the more important part of it, namely, a full restoration of things to the state they were in at the opening of the play; and that he can work better to this end by keeping up his disguise awhile longer. See page 60, note 178.

[414] Meaning, of course, changed, made mad, by his children. So we have *care-crazed* for crazed by care, and *woe-wearied* for wearied by woe.

I doubt not of his temperance.[415]

CORDELIA. Very well.

DOCTOR. Please you, draw near. Louder the music there.[416]

CORDELIA. O my dear father! Restoration hang
    Thy medicine on my lips;[417] and let this kiss
    Repair those violent harms that my two sisters
    Have in thy reverence made!

KENT. Kind and dear princess!

CORDELIA. Had you not been their father, these white flakes
    Had challenged pity of them. Was this a face
    To be opposed against the warring winds?
    To stand against the deep dread-bolted thunder?
    In the most terrible and nimble stroke
    Of quick, cross lightning? to watch—poor perdu!—
    With this thin helm?[418] Mine enemy's dog,
    Though he had bit me, should have stood that night
    Against my fire;[419] and wast thou fain, poor father,
    To hovel thee with swine, and rogues forlorn,
    In short and musty straw? Alack, alack!
    'Tis wonder that thy life and wits at once
    Had not concluded all.[420]—He wakes; speak to him.

DOCTOR. Madam, do you; 'tis fittest.

CORDELIA. How does my royal lord? How fares your majesty?

KING LEAR. You do me wrong to take me out o' the grave:
    Thou art a soul in bliss; but I am bound
    Upon a wheel of fire, that[421] mine own tears
    Do scald like moulten lead.

---

[415] *Temperance* in the classical sense of *self-government* or *self-control*; *calmness*.

[416] Shakespeare considered *soft music* as favourable to sleep. Lear had been thus composed to rest; and now the Doctor desires *louder* music, for the purpose of waking him.

[417] In "Thy medicine," *Thy* may refer either to *father* or to *restoration*. I understand it as referring to *father*: "*May* restoration hang thy medicine on my lips!" Some understand Cordelia as apostrophizing restoration.

[418] This thin *helmet* of "white flakes," or *gray* hair. The allusion is to the forlorn hope of an army, called in French *enfans perdus*; who, among other desperate services, often engage in night-watches. So in Beaumont and Fletcher's *Little French Lawyer*: "I am set here like a *perdu*, to *watch* a fellow that has wronged my mistress."

[419] Verplanck tells us that Jarvis, the American painter-artist, used often to quote this passage as accumulating in the shortest compass the greatest causes of dislike, to be overcome by good—natured pity. "It is not merely the personal enemy, for whom there might be human sympathy, that is admitted to the family fireside, but his dog, and that a dog that had inflicted his own share of personal injury, and that, too, upon a gentle being from whom it was not possible that he could have received any provocation."

[420] *All* may here be taken as going with the subject: "'Tis wonder that thy life and wits had not all concluded"—*ended*—"at once." Probably, however, *all* is here put for *altogether*. Spenser very often has it so.

[421] The Poet very often uses *that* for *so that*, or *insomuch that*.

CORDELIA. Sir, do you know me?

KING LEAR. You are a spirit, I know: when did you die?

CORDELIA. Still, still, far wide!

DOCTOR. He's scarce awake: let him alone awhile.

KING LEAR. Where have I been? Where am I? Fair daylight?
I am mightily abused.[422] I should e'en die with pity,
To see another thus. I know not what to say.
I will not swear these are my hands: let's see;
I feel this pin prick. Would I were assured
Of my condition!

CORDELIA. O, look upon me, sir,
And hold your hands in benediction o'er me:[423]
No, sir, you must not kneel.

KING LEAR. Pray, do not mock me:
I am a very foolish fond old man,
Fourscore and upward, not an hour more nor less;
And, to deal plainly,
I fear I am not in my perfect mind.
Methinks I should know you, and know this man;
Yet I am doubtful for I am mainly[424] ignorant
What place this is; and all the skill I have
Remembers not these garments; nor I know not
Where I did lodge last night. Do not laugh at me;
For, as I am a man, I think this lady
To be my child Cordelia.

CORDELIA. And so I am, I am.

KING LEAR. Be your tears wet? yes, 'faith. I pray, weep not:
If you have poison for me, I will drink it.
I know you do not love me; for your sisters
Have, as I do remember, done me wrong:
You have some cause, they have not.

CORDELIA. No cause, no cause.

KING LEAR. Am I in France?

KENT. In your own kingdom, sir.

KING LEAR. Do not abuse me.

DOCTOR. Be comforted, good madam: the great rage,
You see, is kill'd in him: and yet it is danger
To make him even o'er the time he has lost.[425]

---

[422] To *lead astray* with illusions is an old meaning of *abuse*.

[423] A parent's curse was a dreadful thing with our ancestors; and so Cordelia longs first of all to have her father revoke the curse be pronounced upon her in the opening of the play. She had not learned to act as if "a man were author of himself, and knew no other kin."

[424] Shakespeare sometimes uses *mainly* for *greatly, strongly,* or *mightily*.

[425] "Even o'er the time" here means *try to account for* the time, or to make the last

Desire him to go in; trouble him no more
Till further settling.
CORDELIA. Will't please your highness walk?
KING LEAR. You must bear with me:
Pray you now, forget and forgive: I am old and foolish.[426]

[*Exeunt all but* KENT *and* GENTLEMAN.]

GENTLEMAN. Holds it true, sir, that the Duke of Cornwall was so
slain?
KENT. Most certain, sir.
GENTLEMAN. Who is conductor of his people?
KENT. As 'tis said, the bastard son of Gloucester.
GENTLEMAN. They say Edgar, his banished son, is with the Earl of
Kent in Germany.
KENT. Report is changeable. 'Tis time to look about; the powers of the
kingdom approach apace.
GENTLEMAN. The arbitrement is like to be bloody. Fare you well, sir.
[*Exit.*]
KENT. My point and period will be throughly[427] wrought,
Or well or ill, as this day's battle's fought. [*Exit.*]

ACT V.

SCENE I.

The British Camp near Dover.

[*Enter, with drum and colours,* EDMUND, REGAN, OFFICERS,
SOLDIERS, *and others.*]

EDMUND. Know of the duke if his last purpose hold,
Or whether since he is advised by aught
To change the course.[428] He's full of alteration

---

day of his remembering tally or fit in with the present.—The late Dr. Brigham, with this
speech in his eye, writes as follows: "Although near two centuries and a half have passed
since Shakespeare thus wrote, we have very little to add to his method of treating the
insane as thus pointed out. To produce sleep, and to quiet the mind by medical and moral
treatment, to avoid all unkindness, and, when patients begin to convalesce, to guard, as he
directs, against any thing likely to disturb their minds and to cause a relapse, is now
considered the best and nearly the only essential treatment."

[426] How beautifully the affecting return of Lear to reason, and the mild pathos of his
speeches, prepare the mind for the last sad, yet sweet, consolation of the aged sufferer's
death!—COLERIDGE.

[427] *Throughly* where we should use *thoroughly.*

[428] A military commander is apt, especially on the eve of a battle, to vary his orders

And self-reproving: bring his constant pleasure.

[*To and* OFFICER, *who goes out.*]

To a Gentleman, who goes out
REGAN. Our sister's man is certainly miscarried.
EDMUND. 'Tis to be doubted,[429] madam.
REGAN. Now, sweet lord,
    You know the goodness I intend upon you:
    Tell me,—but truly,—but then speak the truth,
    Do you not love my sister?
EDMUND. In honour'd love.
REGAN. But have you never found my brother's way
    To the forfended place?
EDMUND. That thought abuses you.
REGAN. I am doubtful that you have been conjunct
    And bosom'd with her, as far as we call hers.[430]
EDMUND. No, by mine honour, madam.
REGAN. I never shall endure her: dear my lord,
    Be not familiar with her.
EDMUND. Fear me not:
    She and the duke her husband!

[*Enter, with drum and colours*, ALBANY, GONERIL, *and*
SOLDIERS.]

GONERIL. [*Aside.*] I had rather lose the battle than that sister
    Should loosen him and me.
ALBANY. Our very loving sister, well be-met.—
    Sir, this I hear; the King is come to his daughter,
    With others whom the rigor of our state
    Forced to cry out. Where I could not be honest,
    I never yet was valiant: for this business,
    It toucheth us, as France invades our land,
    Not bolds the King,[431] with others, whom, I fear,
    Most just and heavy causes make oppose.

---

frequently, or to give out an order one hour, and to countermand it the next, as he receives further intelligence of the enemy's movements. Hence, to his subordinates, he often seems not to know his own mind; and his second order appears to *reprove* his first.

[429] Here, as often, *doubted* has the sense of *feared*. The same with *doubtful* in the fifth speech below.

[430] Probably meaning, as far as she has any favours to bestow.

[431] To *bold* was sometimes used as a transitive verb for to *encourage* or *embolden*. Albany means that the invasion touches him, not as it is a befriending of the old King, and aims to reinstate him in the throne, but as it threatens the independence of the kingdom.—*With* has simply the force of and, connecting *others* and *King*.

EDMUND. Sir, you speak nobly.
REGAN. Why is this reason'd?[432]
GONERIL. Combine together 'gainst the enemy;
    For these domestic and particular broils
    Are not the question here.
ALBANY. Let's then determine
    With the ancient of war on our proceedings.[433]
EDMUND. I shall attend you[434] presently at your tent.
REGAN. Sister, you'll go with us?
GONERIL. No.
    REGAN. 'Tis most convenient; pray you, go with us.
GONERIL. [*Aside.*] O, ho, I know the riddle.—I will go.

[*As they are going out, enter* EDGAR *disguised.*]

EDGAR. If e'er your grace had speech with man so poor,
    Hear me one word.
ALBANY. I'll overtake you.—

[*Exeunt all but* ALBANY *and* EDGAR.]

    Speak.
EDGAR. Before you fight the battle, ope this letter.
    If you have victory, let the trumpet sound
    For him that brought it: wretched though I seem,
    I can produce a champion that will prove
    What is avouched there. If you miscarry,
    Your business of the world hath so an end,
    And machination ceases.[435] Fortune love you.
ALBANY. Stay till I have read the letter.
EDGAR. I was forbid it.
    When time shall serve, let but the herald cry,
    And I'll appear again.
ALBANY. Why, fare thee well: I will o'erlook thy paper.

[*Exit* EDGAR.]

---

[432] "Why is this *talked about?*" To *talk*, to *converse* is an old meaning of to *reason*.

[433] This is meant as a proposal, or an order, to hold a council of veteran warriors for determining what course to pursue.

[434] Edmund means that he will soon *join* Albany at his tent, instead of going *along with* him. So the Poet often uses *attend*. In what follows, Goneril lingers to keep with Edmund; and this at once starts Regan's suspicions. When Regan urges Goneril to go along with them, the latter instantly guesses the cause,—the *riddle*,—and replies, "I will go." Very intellectual ladies! "Dragons in the prime, that tear each other in their slime."

[435] "All plottings or designs against your life have an end."

[*Re-enter* EDMUND.]

EDMUND. The enemy's in view; draw up your powers.
    Here is the guess of their true strength and forces
    By diligent discovery; but your haste
    Is now urged on you.
ALBANY. We will greet the time.[436] [*Exit.*]
EDMUND. To both these sisters have I sworn my love;
    Each jealous of the other, as the stung
    Are of the adder. Which of them shall I take?
    Both? one? or neither? Neither can be enjoy'd,
    If both remain alive: to take the widow
    Exasperates, makes mad her sister Goneril;
    And hardly shall I carry out my side,[437]
    Her husband being alive. Now then we'll use
    His countenance for the battle; which being done,
    Let her who would be rid of him devise
    His speedy taking off. As for the mercy
    Which he intends to Lear and to Cordelia,
    The battle done, and they within our power,
    Shall never see his pardon; for my state
    Stands on me to defend,[438] not to debate. [*Exit.*]

SCENE II.

A Field between the two Camps.

[*Alarum within. Enter, with drum and colours,* KING LEAR, CORDELIA, *and their* FORCES, *and exeunt.*]

[*Enter* EDGAR *and* GLOUCESTER.]

EDGAR. Here, father, take the shadow of this tree
    For your good host;[439] pray that the right may thrive:
    If ever I return to you again,
    I'll bring you comfort.
GLOUCESTER. Grace go with you, sir! [*Exit* EDGAR.]

---

[436] "We will be ready for the occasion, or at hand to welcome it."

[437] "I shall hardly be able to make out my game." In the language of the card-table, to *set up a side* was to become partners in a game; and to *carry out a side* was to win or succeed in the game.

[438] The meaning probably is, "for *it* stands upon me," that is, it concerns me, or is incumbent on me, "to defend my state."

[439] A rather strange use of *host*; but Shakespeare has at least two instances of *host* used as a verb for to *lodge*.

[*Alarum and retreat within. Re-enter* EDGAR.]

EDGAR. Away, old man; give me thy hand; away!
　　King Lear hath lost, he and his daughter ta'en:
　　Give me thy hand; come on.
GLOUCESTER. No farther, sir; a man may rot even here.
EDGAR. What, in ill thoughts again? Men must endure
　　Their going hence, even as their coming hither;
　　Ripeness is all.[440] Come on.
GLOUCESTER. And that's true too. [*Exeunt.*]

SCENE III.

The British Camp, near Dover.

[*Enter, in conquest, with drum and colours*, EDMUND, KING
　　LEAR *and* CORDELIA *Prisoners*; OFFICERS, SOLDIERS,
　　&c.]

EDMUND. Some officers take them away: good guard,
　　Until their greater pleasures[441] first be known
　　That are to censure them.
CORDELIA. We are not the first
　　Who, with best meaning, have incurr'd the worst.
　　For thee, oppressed King, am I cast down;
　　Myself could else out-frown false fortune's frown.
　　Shall we not see these daughters and these sisters?
KING LEAR. No, no, no, no! Come, let's away to prison:
　　We two alone will sing like birds i' the cage:
　　When thou dost ask me blessing, I'll kneel down,
　　And ask of thee forgiveness: so we'll live,
　　And pray, and sing, and tell old tales, and laugh
　　At gilded butterflies, and hear poor rogues
　　Talk of court news; and we'll talk with them too,
　　Who loses and who wins; who's in, who's out;[442]
　　And take upon's the mystery of things,
　　As if we were God's spies:[443] and we'll wear out,

---

[440] *Ripeness*, here, is *preparedness* or *readiness*. So Hamlet, on a like occasion, says "the *readiness* is all." And so the phrase, "Like a shock of corn *fully ripe*."

[441] "Their *greater pleasures*" means the pleasure of the *greater persons*.—Here, as usual, to *censure* is to *judge*, to *pass sentence*.

[442] The old King refers to the intrigues and rivalries, the plottings and counter-plottings of courtiers, to get ahead of each other in the sovereign's favour. The swift vicissitudes of *ins* and *outs* in Court life was a common theme of talk in the Poet's time.

In a wall'd prison, packs and sects[444] of great ones,
That ebb and flow by the moon.
EDMUND. Take them away.
KING LEAR. Upon such sacrifices, my Cordelia,
The gods themselves throw incense. Have I caught thee?
He that parts us shall bring a brand from Heaven,
And fire us hence like foxes.[445] Wipe thine eyes;
The goujeers[446] shall devour them, flesh and fell,
Ere they shall make us weep: we'll see 'em starve first.
Come.

[*Exeunt* KING LEAR *and* CORDELIA, *guarded.*]

EDMUND. Come hither, captain; hark.
Take thou this note;[447] [*Giving a paper.*] go follow them to prison:
One step I have advanced thee; if thou dost
As this instructs thee, thou dost make thy way
To noble fortunes: know thou this, that men
Are as the time is: to be tender-minded
Does not become a sword: thy great employment
Will not bear question;[448] either say thou'lt do't,
Or thrive by other means.
CAPTAIN. I'll do't, my lord.
EDMUND. About it; and write happy[449] when thou hast done.
Mark, I say, instantly; and carry it so
As I have set it down.[450]
CAPTAIN. I cannot draw a cart, nor eat dried oats;
If it be man's work, I'll do't. [*Exit.*]

---

[443] Meaning, no doubt, as Heath explains it, "spies commissioned and enabled by God to pry into the most hidden secrets."

[444] *Packs* and *sects* are much the same as what we call political *rings*. The radical meaning of *sect* is *section*; a faction or party.

[445] Alluding to the old practice of smoking foxes out of their holes.

[446] *Goujeer* was the name of what was often spoken of in the Poet's time as the French disease; a disease noted for its effects in *eating away* certain parts of the body.— *Fell* is an old word for skin.

[447] This is a warrant signed by Edmund and Goneril, for the execution of Lear and Cordelia, referred to afterwards.

[448] "The great employment now entrusted to thee will not admit of delay or scrupulous inquiry."

[449] Here, as often, *happy* is *fortunate*; like the Latin *felix*. "*Write* happy" is an old mode of speech, meaning *reckon* or *describe* yourself as a happy man. So, in *Henry IV., Part 2*, i. 2, Falstaff says of the Prince, "and yet he'll be crowing as if he *had writ* man ever since his father was a bachelor."

[450] What this refers to appears afterwards, in Edmund's last speech, "To lay the blame upon her own despair, that she fordid herself."

[*Flourish. Enter* ALBANY, GONERIL, REGAN, OFFICERS, *and* ATTENDANTS.]

ALBANY. Sir, you have shown to-day your valiant strain,[451]
    And fortune led you well: you have the captives
    That were the opposites of this day's strife:
    We do require them of you, so to use them
    As we shall find their merits and our safety
    May equally determine.
EDMUND. Sir, I thought it fit
    To send the old and miserable King
    To some retention and appointed guard;
    Whose age has charms in it, whose title more,
    To pluck the common bosom on his side,
    An turn our impress'd lances[452] in our eyes
    Which do command them. With him I sent the queen;
    My reason all the same; and they are ready
    To-morrow, or at further space, t' appear
    Where you shall hold your session. At this time
    We sweat and bleed: the friend hath lost his friend;
    And the best quarrels, in the heat, are cursed
    By those that feel their sharpness.[453]
    The question of Cordelia and her father
    Requires a fitter place.
ALBANY. Sir, by your patience,
    I hold you but a subject of this war,
    Not as a brother.
REGAN. That's as we list to grace him.
    Methinks our pleasure might have been demanded,
    Ere you had spoke so far. He led our powers;
    Bore the commission of my place and person;
    The which immediacy[454] may well stand up,
    And call itself your brother.

---

[451] *Strain* is repeatedly used in the sense of *turn, aptitude,* or *inborn disposition;* like the Latin *indoles.*

[452] *Lances* for soldiers armed with lances, as, before, *brown-bills* for men armed with battle-axes.—*Impress'd* referring to the men's having been pressed into the service, and received the "press-money."

[453] In a war, even those of the victorious side, those who have the *best* of it, curse the quarrel at first, while they feel its sharpness in the loss of friends, or perhaps in their own wounds.

[454] This apt and forcible word is probably of the Poet's own coinage. Nares says that "the word, so far as is known, is peculiar to this passage." Of course the meaning is, that Edmund has his commission *directly* from her, and not *through* any one else; that is, he is *her* lieutenant, not Albany's. So in *Hamlet* we have "the most *immediate* to the throne." *Commission* is here used in the sense of *authority.*

GONERIL. Not so hot:
  In his own grace he doth exalt himself,
  More than in your addition.
REGAN. In my rights,
  By me invested, he compeers the best.
GONERIL. That were the most, if he should husband you.
REGAN. Jesters do oft prove prophets.
GONERIL. Holla, holla!
  That eye that told you so look'd but a-squint.[455]
REGAN. Lady, I am not well; else I should answer
  From a full-flowing stomach.[456]—General,
  Take thou my soldiers, prisoners, patrimony;
  Dispose of them, of me; the walls are thine:
  Witness the world, that I create thee here
  My lord and master.
GONERIL. Mean you to enjoy him?
ALBANY. The let-alone lies not in your good will.[457]
EDMUND. Nor in thine, lord.
ALBANY. Half-blooded fellow, yes.
REGAN. [*To* EDMUND.] Let the drum strike, and prove my title thine.
ALBANY. Stay yet; hear reason.—Edmund, I arrest thee
  On capital treason; and, in thine attaint,
  This gilded serpent. [*Pointing to* GONERIL.]—For your claim,
  fair sister,
  I bar it in the interest of my wife:
  'Tis she is sub-contracted to this lord,
  And I, her husband, contradict your bans.
  If you will marry, make your loves to me,
  My lady is bespoke.
GONERIL. An interlude![458]
ALBANY. Thou art arm'd, Gloucester: let the trumpet sound:
  If none appear to prove upon thy head
  Thy heinous, manifest, and many treasons,
  There is my pledge: [*Throwing down a glove.*] I'll prove it on thy
  heart,
  Ere I taste bread, thou art in nothing less
  Than I have here proclaim'd thee.

---

[455] Alluding to the proverb, "Love being jealous makes a good eye look *a-squint.*" So in Milton's *Comus*: "And gladly banish *squint suspicion.*"

[456] Here, as often, *stomach* is anger or *resentment.*

[457] Well explained by Ritson: "Albany tells his wife that, however she might want the *power*, she evidently did not want the *inclination*, to prevent the match." In other words, "I see *you* would willingly stop it, if you could." A taunt to his wife, equivalent to "You want him yourself."

[458] This is intended sarcastically; as if Albany had got up a play or a scene for the entertainment of the company.

REGAN. Sick, O, sick!

GONERIL. [*Aside.*] If not, I'll ne'er trust medicine.

EDMUND. There's my exchange: [*Throwing down a glove.*]
>   What in the world he is
>   That names me traitor, villain-like he lies:
>   Call by thy trumpet: he that dares approach,
>   On him, on you, who not? I will maintain
>   My truth and honour firmly.

ALBANY. A herald, ho!

EDMUND. A herald, ho, a herald!

ALBANY. Trust to thy single virtue;[459] for thy soldiers,
>   All levied in my name, have in my name
>   Took their discharge.

REGAN. My sickness grows upon me.

ALBANY. She is not well; convey her to my tent.—

[*Exit* REGAN, *led.*]

[*Enter a* HERALD.]

>   Come hither, herald,—Let the trumpet sound,—
>   And read out this.

CAPTAIN. Sound, trumpet! [*A trumpet sounds.*]

HERALD. [*Reads.*] *If any man of quality or degree within the lists of the army will maintain upon Edmund, supposed Earl of Gloucester, that he is a manifold traitor, let him appear by the third sound of the trumpet: he is bold in his defence.*

EDMUND. Sound! [*First trumpet.*]

HERALD. Again! [*Second trumpet.*]

HERALD. Again! [*Third trumpet.*]

[*Trumpet answers within.*]

[*Enter* EDGAR, *armed, and preceded by a* TRUMPET.]

ALBANY. Ask him his purposes, why he appears
>   Upon this call o' the trumpet.[460]

HERALD. What are you?
>   Your name, your quality? and why you answer
>   This present summons?

---

[459] *Virtue* is used in the old Roman sense; for *valour.*

[460] This is in accordance with the old ceremonial of the trial by combat in criminal cases. So stated in Selden's *Duello*: "The appellant and his procurator first come to the gate. The constable and marshal demand by voice of herald, what he is, and why he comes so arrayed." The same ceremonial is followed in detail in *King Richard II.*, i. 3.

EDGAR. Know, my name is lost;
    By treason's tooth bare-gnawn and canker-bit:
    Yet am I noble as the adversary
    I come to cope.
ALBANY. Which is that adversary?
EDGAR. What's he that speaks for Edmund Earl of Gloucester?
EDMUND. Himself: what say'st thou to him?
EDGAR. Draw thy sword,
    That, if my speech offend a noble heart,
    Thy arm may do thee justice: here is mine.
    Behold, it is the privilege of mine honours,
    My oath, and my profession: I protest,—
    Maugre thy strength, youth, place, and eminence,
    Despite thy victor sword and fire-new fortune,
    Thy valour and thy heart,—thou art a traitor;
    False to thy gods, thy brother, and thy father;
    Conspirant 'gainst this high-illustrious prince;
    And, from the extremest upward of thy head
    To the descent and dust below thy foot,
    A most toad-spotted traitor. Say thou *No*,
    This sword, this arm, and my best spirits, are bent
    To prove upon thy heart, whereto I speak,
    Thou liest.
EDMUND. In wisdom I should ask thy name;[461]
    But, since thy outside looks so fair and warlike,
    And that thy tongue some 'say[462] of breeding breathes,
    What safe and nicely I might well delay[463]
    By rule of knighthood, I disdain and spurn:
    Back do I toss these treasons to thy head;
    With the Hell-hated lie o'erwhelm thy heart;
    Which—for they yet glance by and scarcely bruise,—
    This sword of mine shall give them instant way,
    Where they shall rest for ever.[464]—Trumpets, speak!

[*Alarums. They fight.* EDMUND *falls.*]

---

[461] Because, if his adversary were not of equal rank, Edmund might decline the combat.

[462] "Some '*say*," that is, *assay*, is some *taste*, some *smack*.

[463] That is, "What I might safely well delay if I acted *punctiliously.*" Such is one of the old meanings of *nicely.* If the language be taken strictly, Edmund is made to disdain and spurn the combat; which is clearly just the reverse of his meaning. Perhaps the best way is to understand the language as elliptical: 'The trial, which I might well delay, I disdain and scorn *to delay.*"

[464] *To the place* where they shall rest for ever; that is, in Edgar's heart.

GONERIL. O, save him, save him!—This is practise,[465] Gloucester:
    By th' law of arms thou wast not bound to answer
    An unknown opposite; thou art not vanquish'd,
    But cozen'd and beguiled.
ALBANY. Shut your mouth, dame,
    Or with this paper shall I stop it.—[*To* EDGAR.] Hold, sir!—
    [*To* GONERIL.] Thou worse than any name, read thine own evil:
    No tearing, lady: I perceive you know it.
GONERIL. Say, if I do, the laws are mine, not thine:
    Who can arraign me for't. [*Exit.*]
ALBANY. Most monstrous! O!—
    Know'st thou this paper? [*Offers the letter to* EDMUND.]
GONERIL. Ask me not what I know.[466]
ALBANY. Go after her: she's desperate; govern her.

        [*To an* OFFICER, *who goes out.*]

EDMUND. [*To* EDGAR.] What you have charged me with, that have I done;
    And more, much more; the time will bring it out:
    'Tis past, and so am I. But what art thou
    That hast this fortune on me? If thou'rt noble,
    I do forgive thee.
EDGAR. Let's exchange charity.
    I am no less in blood than thou art, Edmund;
    If more, the more thou hast wrong'd me.
    My name is Edgar, and thy father's son.
    The gods are just, and of our pleasant vices
    Make instruments to plague us:
    The dark and vicious place where thee he got
    Cost him his eyes.
EDMUND. Thou hast spoken right, 'tis true;
    The wheel is come full circle: I am here.
ALBANY. Methought thy very gait did prophesy
    A royal nobleness: I must embrace thee:
    Let sorrow split my heart, if ever I
    Did hate thee or thy father!

---

[465] *Practice*, again, for *plot, stratagem, artifice.* See page 35, note 75. Other instances of the same have occurred in this play; such as "damned *practice*," and "he did bewray his *practice*."

[466] Albany might well ask Edmund, "know'st thou this paper?" for, in fact, Goneril's letter did not reach Edmund; he had not seen it. Edmund, with some spirit of manhood, refuses to make any answers that will criminate or blacken a woman by whom he is loved; and then proceeds, consistently, to answer *Edgar's* charges.

EDGAR. Worthy prince, I know't.
ALBANY. Where have you hid yourself?
    How have you known the miseries of your father?
EDGAR. By nursing them, my lord. List a brief tale;
    And when 'tis told, O, that my heart would burst!
    The bloody proclamation to escape,
    That follow'd me so near,—O, our lives' sweetness!
    That we the pain of death would hourly die,[467]
    Rather than die at once!—taught me to shift
    Into a madman's rags; to assume a semblance
    That very dogs disdain'd: and in this habit
    Met I my father with his bleeding rings,
    Their precious stones new lost: became his guide,
    Led him, begg'd for him, saved him from despair;
    Never,—O fault!—reveal'd myself unto him,
    Until some half-hour past, when I was arm'd:
    Not sure, though hoping, of this good success,[468]
    I ask'd his blessing, and from first to last
    Told him my pilgrimage: but his flaw'd heart,
    Alack, too weak the conflict to support!
    'Twixt two extremes of passion, joy and grief,
    Burst smilingly.
EDMUND. This speech of yours hath moved me,
    And shall perchance do good: but speak you on;
    You look as you had something more to say.
ALBANY. If there be more, more woeful, hold it in;
    For I am almost ready to dissolve,
    Hearing of this.
EDGAR. This would have seem'd a period
    To such as love not sorrow; but another,
    To amplify too much, would make much more,
    And top extremity.[469]

---

[467] "To die hourly with the pain of death," is a periphrasis for to suffer hourly the pain of death.

[468] Here, as in many other places, *success* is *issue* or *result.*—"This good success" refers to the combat with Edmund. Edgar, apprehensive that he might fall, had piously craved his father's benediction on the undertaking. So, in the long run, he who believes in the gods, and fears them, proves too much for the intellectual sceptic and scoffer.

[469] This obscure passage has commonly been set down as corrupt, and I formerly thought it so myself; but I am now satisfied that it is sound. To *amplify* is another instance of the infinitive used gerundively, and is equivalent to *in* or *by amplifying.* See page 65, note 200.—The use of to *top* for to *surpass* is very frequent. See page 30, note 53. So that the sense of the text comes something thus: "To those who are not in love with sorrow, this tale which I have just told would seem to be enough,—seem to require a period, or full stop; but another *such tale added to this,* by amplifying what is already too much, by making that too-much still more, would pass beyond or overtop the utmost limit of distress."—This explanation was suggested to me by Mr. Crosby. *Another* has been

Whilst I was big in clamour came there in a man,
Who, having seen me in my worst estate,
Shunn'd my abhorr'd society; but then, finding
Who 'twas that so endured, with his strong arms
He fastened on my neck, and bellow'd out
As he'd burst Heaven; threw him on my father;
Told the most piteous tale of Lear and him
That ever ear received: which in recounting
His grief grew puissant and the strings of life
Began to crack: twice then the trumpets sounded,
And there I left him tranced.
ALBANY. But who was this?
EDGAR. Kent, sir, the banish'd Kent; who in disguise
Follow'd his enemy King, and did him service
Improper for a slave.

[*Enter a* GENTLEMAN *hastily with a bloody knife.*]

GENTLEMAN. Help, help, O, help!
EDGAR. What kind of help?
ALBANY. Speak, man.
EDGAR. What means that bloody knife?
GENTLEMAN. 'Tis hot, it smokes;
   It came even from the heart of—O, she's dead!
ALBANY. Who dead? speak, man.
GENTLEMAN. Your lady, sir, your lady: and her sister
   By her is poisoned; she hath confess'd it.
EDMUND. I was contracted to them both: all three
   Now marry in an instant.
EDGAR. Here comes Kent.
ALBANY. Produce their bodies, be they alive or dead.—

[*Exit a* GENTLEMAN.]

This judgment of the Heavens, that makes us tremble,
Touches us not with pity.—

[*Enter* KENT.]

   O, is this he?—
The time will not allow the compliment
Which very manners urges.[470]

---

mistaken to mean another *person.* The key to the right sense is in the gerundial infinitive.
   [470] "There is no time now for the interchange of courtesies which mere good-

KENT. I am come
    To bid my King and master aye good night:
    Is he not here?
ALBANY. Great thing of us forgot!—
    Speak, Edmund, where's the King? and where's Cordelia?—
    See'st thou this object, Kent?

[*The bodies of* GONERIL *and* REGAN *are brought in.*]

KENT. Alack, why thus?
EDMUND. Yet Edmund was beloved:
    The one the other poison'd for my sake,
    And after slew herself.
ALBANY. Even so.—Cover their faces.
EDMUND. I pant for life: some good I mean to do,
    Despite of mine own nature. Quickly send—
    Be brief[471] in it—to th' castle; for my writ
    Is on the life of Lear and on Cordelia:
    Nay, send in time.
ALBANY. Run, run, O, run!
EDGAR. To who, my lord? Who hath the office? send
    Thy token of reprieve.
EDMUND. Well thought on: take my sword,
    Give it the captain.
ALBANY. Haste thee, for thy life. [*Exit* EDGAR.]
EDMUND. He hath commission from thy wife and me
    To hang Cordelia in the prison, and
    To lay the blame upon her own despair,
    That she fordid[472] herself.
ALBANY. The gods defend her!—Bear him hence awhile.

[EDMUND *is borne off.*]

[*Re-enter* KING LEAR, *with* CORDELIA *dead in his arms*;
    EDGAR, OFFICER, *and others following.*]

KING LEAR. Howl, howl, howl, howl! O, you are men of stones:
    Had I your tongues and eyes, I'd use them so
    That Heaven's vault should crack. She's gone for ever!
    I know when one is dead, and when one lives;
    She's dead as earth. Lend me a looking-glass;

---

breeding requires, to say nothing of old friendship and affection." The Poet often has *very* in the sense of *mere.*

[471] *Brief* for *quick. Briefly* for *quickly* has occurred before.
[472] To *fordo* signifies to *destroy.*

If that her breath will mist or stain the stone,
Why, then she lives.
KENT. Is this the promised end?
EDGAR. Or image of that horror?[473]
ALBANY. Fall, and cease![474]
KING LEAR. This feather stirs; she lives! if it be so,
It is a chance which does redeem all sorrows
That ever I have felt.
KENT. [*Kneeling.*] O my good master!
KING LEAR. Prithee, away.
EDGAR. 'Tis noble Kent, your friend.
KING LEAR. A plague upon you, murderers, traitors all!
I might have saved her; now she's gone for ever!—
Cordelia, Cordelia! stay a little. Ha!
What is't thou say'st?—Her voice was ever soft,
Gentle, and low, an excellent thing in woman.—
I kill'd the slave that was a-hanging thee.
CAPTAIN. 'Tis true, my lords, he did.
KING LEAR. Did I not, fellow?
I have seen the day, with my good biting falchion
I would have made them skip: I am old now,
And these same crosses spoil me.—Who are you?
Mine eyes are not o' the best: I'll tell you straight.
KENT. If fortune brag of two she loved and hated,
One of them we behold.[475]
KING LEAR. 'Tis is a dull light.[476] Are you not Kent?
KENT. The same,
Your servant Kent: Where is your servant Caius?
KING LEAR. He's a good fellow, I can tell you that;
He'll strike, and quickly too: he's dead and rotten.

---

[473] Kent, more Christian than pagan, recalls those passages of St. Mark in which Christ foretells to His disciples *the end of the world,* and hence his question, "Is this the end of all things, which has been foretold to us?" To which Edgar adds, "Or only a representation of that horror?"

[474] To *cease* is to *die.* Albany, looking on the pains employed by Lear to recover Cordelia, and knowing to what miseries he must survive, when he finds them to be ineffectual, cries out, "Rather fall, and cease to be at once than continue in existence only to be wretched."

[475] This is said, apparently, in answer to Lear's question, "Who are you?" By two, Kent means, of course, himself and the King; by one, himself. In former days, Fortune had indeed seemed to love them both; but, of late, her persecutions have been as bitter as her smiles were sweet before.

[476] The old King is dying; and, as often happens on the approach of death, he mistakes the sudden dimming of his eyes for a defect of light. Goethe's last words are said to have been "More light!" In fact, hardly any thing is more common than for dying people to complain that it is growing dark; and physicians will tell us there is no worse sign than such a calling for light.

KENT. No, my good lord; I am the very man,—
KING LEAR. I'll see that straight.
KENT.—That, from your first of difference and decay,
    Have follow'd your sad steps,—
KING LEAR. You are welcome hither.
KENT.—Nor no man else: all's cheerless, dark, and deadly.
    Your eldest daughters have fordone them selves,
    And desperately are dead.
KING LEAR. Ay, so I think.
ALBANY. He knows not what he says: and vain it is
    That we present us to him.
EDGAR. Very bootless.

    [*Enter an* OFFICER.]

CAPTAIN. Edmund is dead, my lord.
ALBANY. That's but a trifle here.
    You lords and noble friends, know our intent.
    What comfort to this great decay[477] may come
    Shall be applied: for us we will resign,
    During the life of this old majesty,
    To him our absolute power.—[*to* EDGAR *and* KENT.] You, to
      your rights:
    With boot, and such addition as your honours
    Have more than merited. All friends shall taste
    The wages of their virtue, and all foes
    The cup of their deservings.—O, see, see!
KING LEAR. And my poor Fool is hang'd![478] No, no, no life!
    Why should a dog, a horse, a rat, have life,
    And thou no breath at all? Thou'lt come no more,
    Never, never, never, never, never!—
    Pray you, undo this button: thank you, sir.
    Do you see this? Look on her,—look,—her lips,—
    Look there, look there! [*Dies.*]
EDGAR. He faints! My lord, my lord!
KENT. Break, heart; I prithee, break!
EDGAR. Look up, my lord.
KENT. Vex not his ghost: O, let him pass! he hates him much
    That would upon the rack of this tough world
    Stretch him out longer.

---

    [477] "This *great decay*" is Lear. Shakespeare means the same as if he had said, "this piece of decayed royalty." Gloster calls him in a preceding scene "ruin'd piece of nature."

    [478] *Poor fool* was often used as a strong expression of endearment. Here the words refer, not to the Fool, as some have supposed, but to Cordelia, on whose lips the old King is still intent, and dies while he is searching there for indications of life.

EDGAR. He is gone, indeed.
KENT. The wonder is, he hath endured so long:
 He but usurp'd his life.
ALBANY. Bear them from hence.—Our present business
 Is general woe.—[*to* KENT *and* EDGAR.] Friends of my soul, you twain
 Rule in this realm, and the gored state sustain.
KENT. I have a journey, sir, shortly to go;
 My master calls me, I must not say no.[479]
ALBANY. The weight of this sad time we must obey;
 Speak what we feel, not what we ought to say.
 The oldest hath borne most: we that are young
 Shall never see so much, nor live so long.

[*Exeunt, with a dead march.*]

THE END

---

[479] Some question has been made as to Kent's meaning here. He means, to be sure, that all the treasure he had in life is now gone; that the death of his revered and beloved master, and of his "kind and dear Princess," must needs pluck him after. This reminds me of Coleridge's judgment, that "Kent is perhaps the nearest to perfect goodness in all Shakespeare's characters. His passionate affection for, and fidelity to, Lear act on our feelings in Lear's own favour: virtue itself seems to be in company with him."